Imagining Ground Zero

Official and Unofficial Proposals for the World Trade Center Site

Imagining Ground Zero

Suzanne Stephens

with Ian Luna and Ron Broadhurst

Foreword by Robert A. Ivy

Official and Unofficial Proposals for the World Trade Center Site

ARCHITECTURAL
RECORD

RIZZOLI
NEW YORK

First published in the United States of America
in 2004 by
RIZZOLI INTERNATIONAL PUBLICATIONS, INC.
300 Park Avenue South, New York, NY 10010
www.rizzoliusa.com

ISBN: 0-8478-2657-0
LCCN: 2004093314

An *Architectural Record* Book

Designed by Abigail Sturges

Printed and bound in The United States of America

2004 2005 2006 2007 2008 / 10 9 8 7 6 5 4 3 2 1

FRONT COVER Refined master site plan for the World Trade Center Site, Studio Daniel Libeskind (p. 60)

BACK COVER TOP
Collage by Rem Koolhaas/OMA (p. 112)

BACK COVER BOTTOM Aerial perspective of complex scheme by Eisenman Architects (p. 128)

FRONT ENDPAPERS (LEFT) Steel lattice towers seen from the Hudson River, by THINK (p. 67)

FRONT ENDPAPERS (RIGHT) Twin towers seen from the Hudson River, by Foster and Partners (p. 79)

VERSO FACING HALF-TITLE PAGE Megastructure as seen while looking up from the footprints of the former WTC towers, by United Architects (p. 76)

PAGES 2 AND 3 Digital rendering by Marwan Al-Sayed, WTC scheme for "A New World Trade Center: Design Proposals" invitational exhibition at Max Protetch Gallery, January 17–February 16, 2002 (p. 159)

RECTO FACING PAGE 224 Perspective view east, by Morphosis (p. 120)

BACK ENDPAPERS (LEFT) Megastructure at night, by Nox (p. 136)

BACK ENDPAPERS (RIGHT) A Tribute in Light, by Bennett, Bonevardi, Nash-Gould, LaVerdiere, and Myoda (p. 183)

Contents

Preface

When we began gathering material for this visual history of various proposals for Ground Zero, we decided the compendium had to include unofficial schemes as well as the official ones. Granted, a number of the unofficial ones are pipe dreams, unrealizable in our lifetimes. But we were undeterred in our gleanings, even when one New York architect of large-scale projects asked why his firm should want to be in the book with so many fantasies. We responded, "All of it is fantasy—until the first building is built. Then we get the first glimpse of reality."

In presenting these schemes, some more fantastical than others, we first separated the unofficial ones from the official proposals executed under the aegis of the Lower Manhattan Development Corporation and the Port Authority of New York and New Jersey. Then we distinguished the unofficial schemes according to the categories of their sources, such as the press-generated responses (*New York* magazine, *New York Times Magazine*), the Max Protetch exhibition "A New World Trade Center: Design Proposals," and the independent schemes, where proposals were usually self-generated by individual architects and designers.

Besides being organized according to the sources, the book is arranged chronologically. But the chronology moves back in time, from where we are now. So we begin with the official schemes and present the ones that seem to be closest to being realized today (April 2004). Then we move back in time, with both official and unofficial schemes, gradually arriving at the first round of proposals executed for the Max Protetch exhibition in January 2002. We see this as an archaeological dig where we sift through the layers of the process to see how the fantasy and reality intersected in this compressed amount of time.

Foreword

No one asked for such an outpouring of creativity. Least of all the staff of *Architectural Record*, many of whom were gathered on the thirty-seventh floor of 55 Water Street on September 11, 2001. On that brilliant blue day, we stood transfixed, when, in a flash, two aircraft slammed into the iconic Twin Towers directly across from our line of sight. We felt the blows, and scrambled into the streets and up onto the Brooklyn Bridge. Then, with a malignant rumble, the unimaginable happened when the first (south) tower collapsed in 12 seconds, taking a large toll in human life and in our collective understanding. What, we wondered, had happened to our world? The question reverberated and haunts us still.

For *Architectural Record*, the first stories on the World Trade Center attacks appeared on our Web site on September 12. Shortly thereafter, although our October issue was ready for printing, the staff mobilized, tore up previous work, and added significant content to the upcoming issue. That coverage has continued regularly until this date, including monthly news stories, critiques and analyses of proposed schemes, and editorials that pressed for change. We also served as a kind of repository for architectural proposals and schemes for our readership as we began to advocate for excellence in the rehabilitation of the site.

We were not alone. The entire press quickly realized that a sea change had occurred in the role of architectural design as unrequested, unanticipated ideas began to filter into media offices throughout the country. The first trickle arrived in early fall, some predictable, some quiescent, some visionary, and all transcending age, education, and station, coming from young schoolchildren to great designers. It became clear that the question raised by the erasure of the World Trade Center demanded an answer: What should replace it?

If any good could come from such a cataclysm, it would be this worldwide intellectual and spiritual response. In metaphysical terms, the embedded energy represented by the 110-story towers, the physicality embodied by the acres of concrete and steel, underwent transubstantiation, a metamorphosis in which solid matter was changed by the explosions of fuel-laden aircraft into power. Born in an act of aggression, ironically, this power was transformed into positive ideas, both interrogatory and declarative. What physical monument should memorialize the lives lost? What new structures, if any, should replace the former World Trade Center complex? How high should tall buildings reach in the coming years? What should be the relationship of any new buildings to the future of lower Manhattan? And, for

the grieving, how should the determination of remembrance be acknowledged? The trickle soon became a flood.

But the question of how or where the upwelling designs could be viewed had yet to be addressed. Although he faced derision and skepticism in the critical community for acting so early, the gallery owner Max Protetch mounted a show of architectural ideas, with the help of *Architectural Record* and others, in January 2002 that provided a clue into the depth of feeling. The Protetch show underscored the depth of popular hunger for answers to the existential questions raised in the earlier tragedy, coupled with the ascendance of design in the public consciousness. From that evening to this day, television, newspapers, and Web sites began to acknowledge that lower Manhattan needed what architecture and planning offered. The architect, and architecture, for once, took center stage.

Throughout 2002, numerous public forums throughout New York City, spurred by groups, including New York New Visions, the Civic Alliance to Rebuild Downtown New York, Downtown Our Town, the Municipal Arts Society, and the Architectural League, along with universities and museums, debated the outcome for Ground Zero, as the site quickly came to be called. A major benchmark of the expression of public opinion occurred on July 20, 2002, at a Town Hall meeting called "Listening to the City," convened by the Civic Alliance at the Javits Center and attended by over four thousand people. On that day, tables of ten persons listened to the presentation of the first-round proposed master plans for the World Trade Center site, then debated, voted, and rejected the lot. The plebiscite spoke and with a unified voice said, "No."

The meeting was noteworthy, not so much for its game-show format or its pseudodemocratic structure as for the discussions it provoked. Scattered among the tables throughout the vast center was a demographic sampling of the city: schoolteachers, firefighters, university professors, professional planners, family members who had lost loved ones, and intellectuals. The result might have been cacophony; yet at each table, with varying levels of articulation, the topic was clear, and clearly debated, as everyone engaged the intricacies of urban design.

ABOVE The audience for the *Architectural Record* panel discussion "Waiting for Ground Zero," at the McGraw-Hill auditorium, New York, January 7, 2003

The distinction between urban design and architecture became subsequently blurred, however, when the Lower Manhattan Development Corporation and the Port Authority of New York and New Jersey called for an "Innovative Design Study." While new master plans were ostensibly the subject of the invited competition, few proposed schemes actually knit a solution into New York's urban fabric. When seven teams of world-renowned architects presented their schemes at the freshly restored Winter Garden of the World Financial Center on December 18, 2002, the debates concerned the three-dimensional and formal characteristics of the schemes as much as their urban fit.

Critics argued whether Norman Foster's sculptural twin towers could be built in increments, or whether Daniel Libeskind's vertiginous assemblage captured the zeitgeist of present-day New York; whether the scheme from the so-called "New York" team (Richard Meier, Peter Eisenman, Charles Gwathmey, Steven Holl) overwhelmed the skyline, and the relationship of the United Architects proposal to Italian visionary city planning. Though today's arguments assert the primacy of master-planning throughout the process, the prevailing argument from the period is graphic, not verbal. One picture told the story: on the front page of *USA Today*, twin towers conceived by the THINK team glowed against a moonlit Manhattan—a poetic, sculptural, clearly architectural idea.

Through these months, *Architectural Record* has not only followed the unfolding drama, but led. In a hitherto unprecedented way, its editors have served as panelists, moderators, and provocateurs (including the first critical look at the Innovative Design Study, "Waiting for Ground Zero," held on January 7, 2003). We

have commented on the World Trade Center progress for magazines, newspapers, television, and radio. In September 2002, *Architectural Record* took an active role in the Architectural Biennale in Venice (for which I was the commissioner of the United States Pavilion). We helped organize an exhibition, "World Trade Center: Past, Present, and Future," which featured proposals from the Max Protetch exhibition of the preceding January, along with photographs by Joel Meyerowitz. A month before, *Architectural Record*'s award-winning August 2002 issue, "The Architecture of Remembrance," explored the shifting nuances that define monuments, memorials, and meaning, illustrated with contemporary examples from around the world. And now, with Suzanne Stephens as author, we present this book as a visual chronicle of an unparalleled moment.

Just as no one sought the surfeit of creative ideas, we editors did not seek a public role but were thrust into it by events. What you hold in your hand, a document of the wealth of architectural and urbanistic ideas to emerge over the last two and a half years, came about through hardship, human loss, and pain. Through acts of human will as well as the vagaries of fate, architecture lay at the intersection of past and future—as plan, aspiration, and resolution. While the outcome of the final solutions for the site remains unclear, clouded as it is by political and economic machinations endemic to any work in New York, *Architectural Record* will continue to cast a searchlight, and, when necessary, to point.

Robert A. Ivy
Editor in Chief
Architectural Record

Time Line

Rebuilding the World Trade Center Site
after September 11, 2001

OFFICIAL

Lower Manhattan Development Corporation and Port Authority of New York and New Jersey

May 16, 2002
Shortlist of architectural, planning, and engineering teams determined for concept studies of World Trade Center site

May 22, 2002
Beyer Blinder Belle selected as master planners for WTC site

July 16, 2002
Beyer Blinder Belle presents six concept plans

July 20, 2002
Town Hall meeting at Javits Center on Beyer Blinder Belle plans

September 26, 2002
Seven finalists announced for Innovative Design Study competition; they have eight weeks to work on proposals

December 18, 2002
Seven teams present nine proposals

February 4, 2003
Studio Daniel Libeskind and THINK (Rafael Viñoly, Frederic Schwartz, Shigeru Ban, Ken Smith, et al.) selected as second-stage finalists

February 27, 2003
Studio Daniel Libeskind selected winner, Innovative Design Study

July 31, 2003
Santiago Calatrava, DMJM + Harris, and STV Group (Downtown Design Partnership) selected by Port Authority of New York and New Jersey to design WTC Transportation Hub

September 17, 2003
Studio Daniel Libeskind releases "Refined Master Site Plan"

November 19, 2003
Eight finalists for memorial competition selected

December 19, 2003
Freedom Tower, by David Childs of SOM, with Daniel Libeskind as collaborating architect through initial phases, unveiled

January 6, 2004
Michael Arad and Peter Walker announced as winners of memorial competition

January 14, 2004
Revised memorial scheme by Arad and Walker released

January 22, 2004
Calatrava, DMJM + Harris, and STV Group release design for WTC Transportation Hub

UNOFFICIAL

January 17–February 16, 2002
"A New World Trade Center: Design Proposals" invitational exhibition, held at Max Protetch Gallery, New York

September 8, 2002
New York Times Magazine presents its ideas for enlarged site, curated by Herbert Muschamp

September 16, 2002
New York magazine presents its proposals, organized by Joseph Giovannini

Fantasy Intersects with

Suzanne Stephens

Out of the horrific tragedy of September 11, 2001, has emerged a stunning, imaginative outpouring of design. The range of original responses to the need to rebuild the World Trade Center site in New York City is impressive. That the cornucopia of visions should be prompted by such heartbreaking loss of lives and shocking devastation is a hauntingly cruel irony. But after this cataclysmic event, many architects felt that they must do *something*, and that is to do what they know best—design. Theirs was an optimistic resolve: that innovative architecture may offer a way to heal ourselves as well as Manhattan's mangled downtown.

The visual compilation of schemes shown on the following pages may ensure this effort is not forgotten. This pictorial history presents responses to official, government-sponsored competitions and commissions, as well as unofficial solicitations for presentations organized by the *New York Times Magazine*, *New York* magazine, and the Max Protetch Gallery. In addition, a cluster of proposals is presented that were independently volun-

teered to the public and the press, along with some submissions to the official memorial competition, which were not premiated. Not all the examples of the staggering array of imaginative efforts are included in this visual survey, for reasons of space and impediments that could not be resolved in time for this publication. In terms of the "independent" schemes presented as the last chapter, we made a selection of certain ones that had come to our attention and presented intriguing ideas about the site. Needless to say, many more schemes are out there.

The Aura of the Competition

The officially sponsored competitions that generated so many of the schemes in the book have elicited a massive amount of attention. The competitions vary in their nature, however, and it should be remembered that the design for the largest component to appear so far in the World Trade Center rebuilding process did not result from a competition: the 1,776-foot-high

Reality at Ground Zero

Freedom Tower by David Childs of Skidmore, Owings & Merrill (the design architect and project manager) and Daniel Libeskind (as collaborating architect through concept and schematic design phases). Childs had been hired to renovate the towers by the developer Larry Silverstein when he first acquired the lease to the World Trade Center shortly before the complex was destroyed; Libeskind was brought into the design process on a short-term contract in response to public expectations that he, as the master planner of the site, would be involved in the design of the tallest building. The World Trade Center Transportation Hub, being designed by Santiago Calatrava, DMJM + Harris, and STV Group, was won through a limited competition sponsored only by the Port Authority. Through a Request for Qualifications procedure, teams submitted credentials to the Port Authority, then a shortlist of three teams was whittled down from the entrants, and finally Calatrava's group, called the Downtown Design Partnership, was selected. The Request for Qualifications procedure, where the architects submit only their portfolios, not actual

design concepts, was used for the first two stages of the selection of the master planner for the site. Only in the second round of the Innovative Design Study did teams start proposing design schemes, after the list of candidates was narrowed to seven teams. As a distinctly separate approach, the memorial competition was open and based on a Request for Proposal process, with an outside jury selecting the final and winning designs. Needless to say, the final stages of the Innovative Design Study and the memorial competition had a galvanizing effect on the press and public: the haze hanging over the entire "transparent" official selection process was converted into the aura of a sports event. Not since the Chicago Tribune Tower competition of 1922, for a headquarters sponsored by the newspaper, had such controversy surrounded architectural competitions in the United States, notorious for being laggard in this area when compared to the attention given to architectural competitions in Europe. With the Chicago Tribune Tower, only 263 design proposals were submitted, compared to the 406 responses to the RFQ for the

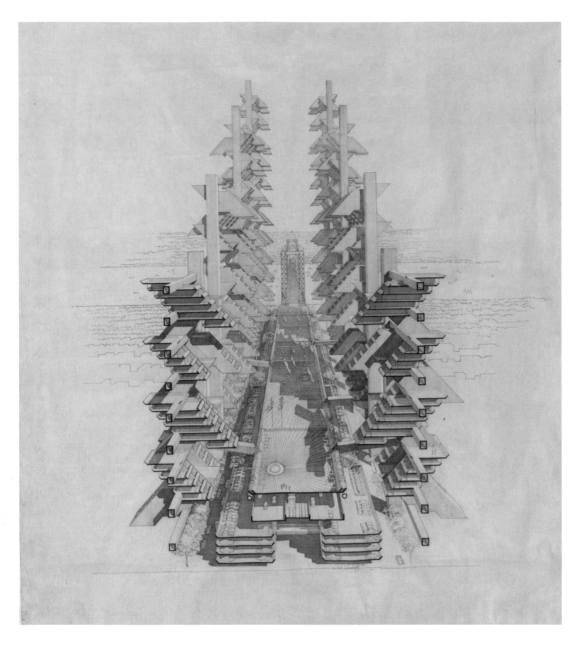

World Trade Center Innovative Design Study, or the 5,201 designs submitted for the memorial competition. Although the unofficial proposals sponsored by the press and cultural organizations shown in the following pages are not competitions per se, the sense that this is all one big contest still permeates the air.

The architects and artists, often with the help of planners and engineers, have produced a compelling array of schemes, which represent a cross section of current design thinking on a global scale. Many of the schemes are impractical beyond our wildest visions. But in this digital age, computer drawings enable the schemes to look as real as if they were in our backyard. The defiant optimism they project about their worth and the possibility of ultimate realization comes through in numerous images. Why optimistic? Perhaps now that Americans have been dragged into the terrorism of everyday life that has long afflicted our counterparts in other parts of the globe, we need a little optimism. Architects in particular must be optimistic: They know they have neither legal power (as do governors and mayors) nor economic power (as do real estate developers) to make their mark. They only have their ideas.

Influence of the Image

Instead of power, architects have influence. This influence depends on their being able to persuade through visual concepts rendered with drawings, models, and, of course, computer-generated design. If these ideas have little bearing on reality, the images nevertheless provide the seed for future thought, and not just about form, for the seed of imagination is necessary to feed the constructive process. Fantastic images can postulate alternate transportation means, new building technologies, varied urban agglomerations, or different programmatic activities. Once implanted, the ideas can lie dormant, but the images linger in books, magazines, and in the not-so-conscious public memory. At some point they might reemerge from an architect's creative impulse, brought to life for a particular occasion, with the right building techniques and program. We might call this the Finsterlin effect. The German Expressionist Hermann Finsterlin's biomorphic drawings of the early 1920s could be argued to have anticipated the organicism of Frank Gehry's Guggenheim Bilbao museum (1997) and Walt Disney Concert Hall (2002). Finsterlin, not trained as an architect, never built anything, and, indeed, his contemporaries felt that the ideas would be ruined by being physically realized. But as C. J.

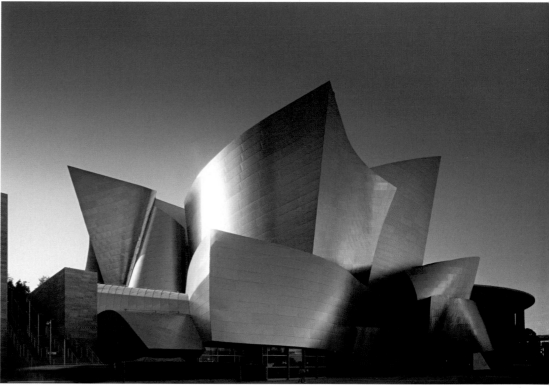

Blaauw argued in an issue of *Wendigen* magazine devoted to Finsterlin in 1924, "When we stay with Finsterlin in the wonderful world of his architectonic imagination, we shall be reminded of our boldest dreams, in which we thought ourselves free from past and present, and then when we return to our own architectural world, we shall perhaps carry along something of our own. . . ."[1]

Now with computer-aided graphics and advances in construction technology, it is possible to realize past utopian visions. One era's fantasy is almost another's reality. Of course it might seem that gathering visual images of hypothetical urban forms is hopelessly naive—trading in fantasy, and succumbing to myth. More than forty years ago, Daniel J. Boorstin complained that the "language of images" had replaced ideals.[2] This was even before French cultural theorist Jean Baudrillard began attacking the cultural emphasis on the image in the late 1960s.[3] Boorstin was using *image* to refer to a contrived presentation of self, as in "corporate image," and castigated American society for being so distracted by image that it could not pursue ideals. This contemporary compilation of architectural images may appear to pander to such distractions: It does not attempt to present all the realistic planning solutions, including land-use

patterns, transit infrastructure, and designs for streets and plazas that have been generated in response to September 11. Nor is this book a behind-the-scenes investigation about the nature of the planning process. Quite a few schemes are under-developed; some seek mainly to comment on political and social issues of the present.

Indeed, the projected schemes vary greatly in the parameters to which they adhere: many follow official programs for planning the site or designing the memorial, while others are guided only by the imaginations of their authors. For that reason they are organized according to the sponsoring entity, whether it is a government agency, the press, or an art gallery.

Time is another factor. Those designs executed in the brief span between September 11, 2001, and the opening of the Max Protetch show "A New World Trade Center: Design Proposals" on January 17, 2002, bear their marks of the short time frame. By contrast, those Innovative Design Study schemes developed in consultation with Lower Manhattan Development Corporation officials over the course of two months demonstrate the benefits of slightly more time, more money, and more distance from the catastrophic event. Lack of time has been one of the major

complaints about all these efforts. Not even the architects for the most developed proposals had enough time to mull and stew, to think, toss out, reject, and come back and redo. So why bother? The answer: This was the time to expose the public to possibilities available before the wheels of business as usual were able to start churning away. A number of government engineers, politicians, and community interest groups had to confront these visions no matter how new (and scary) they were. While the concern with images has been criticized for ignoring facts about finance, transit needs, rights-of-way for transportation underground, property owners' rights, and the public's desires, the images can have their own raisons d'être.

What is seen in the following compilation reflects the thinking of international and American architects and designers, whether they are avant-garde, already established, or on the way up. The buildings they propose often suggest new solutions, some of which take on animate forms, vertically or horizontally, that bend, curl, and seem to grow. Others seem so diaphanous that they almost disappear in the clouds, or, in the case of Peter Eisenman's scheme for *New York* magazine, are infused with a flowing energy that dematerializes before the eye. Some of the responses postulate programs for new buildings (such as a world peace center); some come up with new ways to devise a program, such as Winka Dubbeldam's scheme for the Max Protetch exhibition, in which an interactive electronic environment allows people the opportunity to determine their own work

and living spaces. Tom Kovac, also in the Protetch show, presents a biomorphic design in which form is generated from data based on new organizational relationships within the complex. We also see a range of urban planning strategies developed, resulting in a variegated imagery, such as the ones Michael Sorkin has devised both for the Max Protetch exhibition and, later, independently. Many of the proposals stress burying the six-lane highway called West Street, which cuts the WTC site off from Battery Park City. A number of others see this rebuilding process as the opportunity to restore some of Manhattan's grid. Sustainability is another theme that recurs in many solutions, and energy-saving windmills seem to be the favored apparatus to have at the top of the tower. Indeed, in the winter of 2004, the Municipal Art Society sponsored an open competition for Green Ground Zero proposals. Three finalists will be chosen from twenty-eight entries submitted by architects, artists, and environmentalists, among others.

A number of schemes, particularly early ones, emphasized horizontality. The vertical skyscraper was too dangerous. Many considered the day of the skyscraper to be over. Some, such as those by Tadao Ando and Ellsworth Kelly, represent symbolic statements about this condition. Yet the majority of architects (and officials involved in planning) who drew up designs for Ground Zero kept the skyscraper. As America's invention, the skyscraper was too significant. And it was too much a part of New York City's history.

The Skyscraper's Hold on Lower Manhattan

It is arresting to consider how many schemes for the World Trade Center site include skyscrapers, in spite of the fear of tall buildings that naturally arose after September 11. Following the collapse of the Twin Towers, the sentiment seemed to prevail that towers over sixty-five stories should not be erected. Yet by 2002, the Lower Manhattan Development Corporation was urging that "skyline elements" be included in the Innovative Design Study. A skyline element is still a skyscraper, even if its top is not occupied. Today the projected towers provide floors that can be occupied up to about sixty-five stories, with the rest of the tower turned over to energy-saving devices and other such programs.

New York's fascination with and attraction to the skyscraper has a complex history, intertwined with the growth of downtown Manhattan. Depending on how you define the term *skyscraper*, New York City could claim to be its birthplace. Chicago had the steel frame, but with the installation of the first passenger elevator in 1857, New York was soon involved in early height wars. While Chicago had the world's tallest building for a time (Burnham & Root's Masonic Temple designed 1891–92) at a 274-foot height, New York quickly spawned a cluster of record-breaking skyscrapers: from the St. Paul Building in lower Manhattan, designed by George Post in 1895–98 and 315 feet high; to the Park Row Building nearby, designed by R. H.

Robertson in 1896–99, which soared to 391 feet; to Ernest Flagg's 620-foot-high Singer Tower, also built downtown in 1908, at Broadway and Liberty Street (now demolished). Although the 700-foot-high Metropolitan Life Insurance Tower, designed by Napoleon Le Brun, finished in 1909, was located uptown at Twenty-third Street, the Woolworth Building by Cass Gilbert, back downtown, soared to 792 feet when it was completed in 1913.[4] For various reasons (soil conditions, resistant fire insurers, zoning laws, economics), Chicago couldn't keep up with New York's skyscrapers.[5]

Downtown/Midtown Competition

It is not surprising that most of New York's skyscrapers were concentrated downtown. As is well known, for much of its history New York City's center was in the lower part of Manhattan, where its port created an active mercantile capital, which functioned as a financial center and the seat of city government. By the mid-nineteenth century, residential sections had been gradually pushed out by commerce (with retail trailing along), but it was not until the 1930s that the doubling of New York's city centers was clear. By then Midtown was the home of the iconic Chrysler Building (1930) by William Van Alen, the Empire State Building by Shreve, Lamb & Harmon (1929–31), and Rockefeller Center (1932–40) by Reinhard & Hofmeister, Corbett, Harrison & MacMurray, Raymond Hood, and Godley & Fouilhoux.

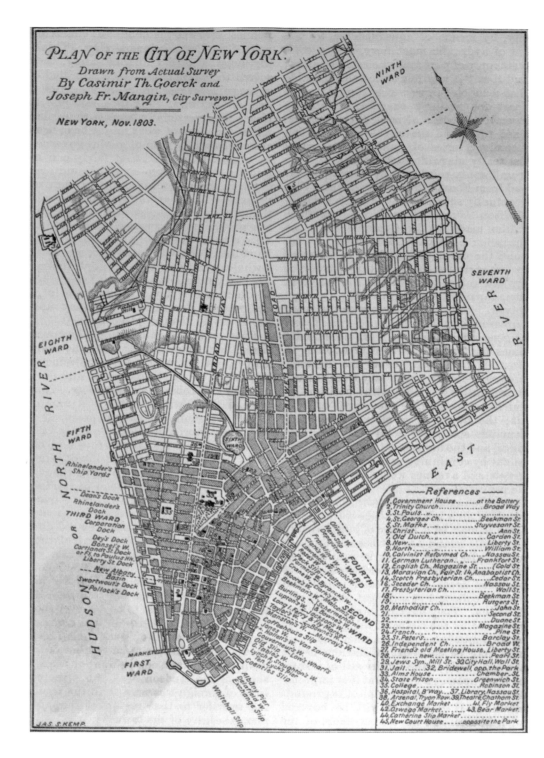

LEFT Plan of lower Manhattan as the "center" of New York, 1803

OPPOSITE, TOP Lower Manhattan looking north, 1958

OPPOSITE, BOTTOM Site plan of World Trade Center area before superblock is created

By the 1940s, Midtown was becoming *the* center; downtown was a B-list location. Rockefeller Center, finished in the 1940s, gave a center to the center: its agglomeration of low-, mid-, and high-rise buildings around an open space, its continuation and supplementing of streets to the city grid effectively reinforced Midtown's hegemony. Soon tourists could go downtown to Wall Street and the Statue of Liberty nearby, but they hadn't come to "The City" until they visited Rockefeller Center.

After World War II, modern architecture arrived in Midtown. Architectural distinction came in the form of the Lever House by SOM (1952), the Seagram Building by Mies van der Rohe and Philip Johnson (1958), the granite-clad CBS building by Eero Saarinen (1963), and the United Nations headquarters (1947–53), with Wallace Harrison as chief architect. Soon the glass-and-steel corporate knockoffs followed. Midtown had it made.

Dreary Downtown's Dilemma

John D. Rockefeller Jr. dreamed up Rockefeller Center, which was carried out with the help of his son Nelson. By the 1950s, Nelson's brother, David, a banker, decided to bolster the moribund financial, insurance, and civic dullsville of lower Manhattan, and keep companies from drifting away to Midtown. Downtown's once vibrant working waterfront had been altered by the introduction of containerized shipping. The piers were inactive, and only a few new buildings were going up. Then David Rockefeller, as vice chairman of the expanding Chase Manhattan Bank, announced Chase would build its new headquarters downtown. Designed by Skidmore, Owings & Merrill, it was finished in 1960.[6]

Although the revitalization of lower Manhattan seemed to be on the way, David Rockefeller was not taking chances. He had

organized the Downtown–Lower Manhattan Association in 1956, and by 1960 had proposed a World Trade Center, a combination of offices and a hotel with a trade or art exhibition hall and central securities exchange building. The center was located along the East River, and the design was executed by Skidmore, Owings & Merrill.

Then the Port Authority of New York and New Jersey bounced back with its own report, and its own group of architects (Richard Adler, of Brodsky, Hopf & Adler working with consultants Gordon Bunshaft of SOM, Wallace Harrison, and Edward Durell Stone). By 1962, the Port Authority had taken over the project and moved it to the west part of the island, in order to take advantage of its own Trans-Hudson (PATH) railroad holdings. Minoru Yamasaki and Emery Roth & Sons were named the architects. The complex, on a 16-acre site, bounded by West, Vesey, Church, and Liberty streets, featured a 5-acre plaza and seven buildings,

with the two 110-story, 1,350-foot-high World Trade Center towers to be the tallest in the world. As a superblock the ensemble would long be vilified for its destruction of the urban scale imposed by New York City's grid. Ironically, the later collapse of the towers would make it harder to bring the grid fully back to its pre-1960s status, owing to the desire to preserve the WTC footprints as part of a memorial.

The World Trade Center also destroyed a vibrant low-profile commercial ghetto for electronics shops known as Radio Row. Politics and family had won out: Nelson Rockefeller, now the New York State governor, enabled the Port Authority to build 10 million square feet for the entire complex, more than the amount that David had originally proposed.[7] Other politicians and agencies joined in the expansion, and excavated soil was used as landfill to create Battery Park City, a development of apartments and more skyscrapers.[8]

OPPOSITE World Trade Center, Minoru Yamasaki and Emery Roth & Sons, photographed 1978

RIGHT, TOP Plaza, World Trade Center, Yamasaki and Roth, photographed 1978

RIGHT, BOTTOM Site plan, World Trade Center

Owing to the loose soil, the foundations for the 200-foot-square, steel-frame structures had to extend 70 feet below grade to be anchored into bedrock. A 3-foot-thick slurry wall of bentonite (a clay made from volcanic ash) formed a 3,500-foot-long "bathtub" around the site to keep the Hudson River water from seeping in.[9] The towers themselves were designed to be framed tubes, where narrowly spaced exterior columns carried part of the load. With structural cores for elevators and stairs, the actual office floors could be free of columns. The design of the exterior steel columns, clad in aluminum, was gussied-up modern: arches at the base (evoking Gothic, Venetian, and Islamic motifs) fused into a strong vertical pinstripe pattern. When the designs were released in 1966, Ada Louise Huxtable, writing in the *New York Times*, asked, "Who's afraid of the big, bad buildings? Everyone. Because there are so many things about gigantism that we just don't know." Presciently, she ended her piece, "The Trade Center towers could be the start of a new skyscraper age or the biggest tombstones in the world."[10]

In spite of extensive reportage on the buildings as they were going up, by the time the towers had been completed, the critical response was tepid. In 1973, Huxtable wrote again in the *Times*, "These are big buildings but they are not great architecture."[11] Gerald Allen, writing in *Architectural Record* in 1974, pointed out that the main entry was from underground: if office workers wanted to enter from the plaza, they had to ascend a half-flight of stairs, and then take an escalator back down to the main floor.[12]

In a rival (now defunct) architecture magazine, *Architectural Forum*, this author wrote a satire in 1973, "W.T.C. 2023." It was intended as a criticism, not only of the planning process that allowed the megaliths to be built, but as a tongue-in-cheek prediction that the critical disdain for the towers would be reversed in fifty years, when the buildings were eligible for landmarking.[13]

Not surprisingly, Italian Marxist architecture critics and historians found it wanting as well. In 1973 (translated in 1979), Manfredo Tafuri scornfully assessed the new "super-skyscraper"—the World Trade Center towers, as well as the John Hancock and Sears towers in Chicago: "Neither technological revision nor urban planning logic underlies these undertakings." Arguing that until the 1940s at least there was some sort of "integration between the skyscraper and the metropolis," Tafuri proclaimed that "the relationship between skyscraper and city has been definitively broken."[14]

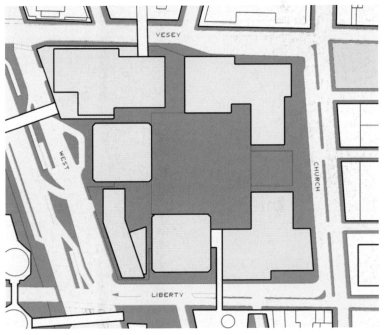

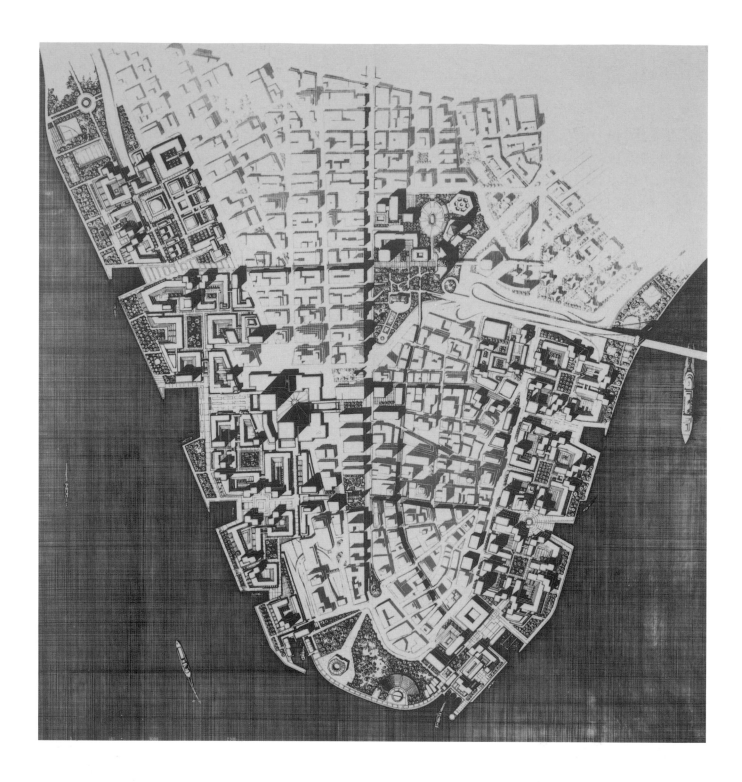

From the WTC Outward: Reclaiming the Waterfront

During the period when the World Trade Center complex was being built, a group of architects began preparing a plan for the downtown area in 1964 that placed the World Trade Center in a more developed context. The group, outside consultants to the Department of City Planning, included architects and planners Wallace, McHarg, Roberts, and Todd, along with Whittlesey, Conklin, and Rossant, plus transportation consultants Alan M. Voorhees & Associates. Their report, *The Lower Manhattan Plan*, released in 1966, became the basis for the city's own *Plan for New York City*, produced in 1969.[15]

The original idea behind the plan had been to create a civic center downtown, where city government offices would be grouped, which included a monumental building designed by Edward Durell Stone. Soon this idea was jettisoned, and what emerged was an urban plan for regaining use of the waterfront

by the community, and the creation of residential living downtown. The plan, which was accompanied by architecturally detailed drawings, placed office towers inland, giving way to low- and mid-rise apartment megastructural blocks and urban parks and promenades around coves at the water's edge. While accepting the World Trade Center site as it was, it nevertheless offered ways to connect the superblock back to Manhattan.

The reception to the plan was responsive: When John Lindsay became the mayor in 1965, he instituted the Office of Lower Manhattan Development to oversee it and draw up a plan for the whole district.[16] Like other such offerings, it was not literally adopted, but remained in the mind's eye of planners, where it maintained a degree of influence.

Meanwhile, the Twin Towers continued to gain in status as symbolic markers of New York's determined claim to be the capital of the twentieth century. Battery Park City's residential high-rises and office buildings (called the World Financial Center) and other office buildings brought the area back to life. Downtown, the second sister to Midtown for so long, was coming into its own. Until September 11.

Anxiety, Desire, and Height

After September 11, 2001, a good many people responding to polls seemed to want to rebuild the towers as they were, in defiance of the terrorists. In fact, Team Twin Towers, a private advocacy group led by film and television executive Randy Warner, with the assistance of architect Ken Gardner, suggested replicating the Twin Towers as they were, only with more structural stability. They proposed fireproof ceramic polymer coatings around columns, concrete floor beams and stairs, bioterrorism sensors, and various other options. Still others argued that towers should not reach over sixty stories in height; anything higher was surely a target for future attacks. In terms of the continuing droopy real estate market, that number still sounds reasonable, although Freedom Tower is designed to

have sixty-eight stories occupied, including the mechanical space, conference rooms, and restaurants on the top floors.

Generally, it seems New Yorkers do not want to sacrifice their skyline. Even if a skyscraper is not occupied in its upper reaches, it should at least have a towering "skyline element," in the words of the Lower Manhattan Development Corporation, such as a transmission tower, or a structure containing energy-saving devices, such as wind turbines. Adam Gopnik, writing in the *The New Yorker*, expressed the psychological appeal of this American invention: "Now that tall buildings are for the first time fragile in our memory and imagination, susceptible to a morning's doom, we fill them with feelings, and accept that they are representations of our hopes, rather than wrappers of our necessities."[17]

Skyscrapers embody our dreams and fantasies about the future. The attraction to skyscrapers—not something Lewis Mumford, who hated the race toward tallness and density, would have condoned—is difficult for the rest of us to shrug off. The sky-

scraper has become as much a part of the American identity as any other artifact. And that is perhaps why we are reluctant to give them up. Non-American architects are already designing some of the highest and most technologically daring skyscrapers, often outside the United States. While American architects Cesar Pelli, Kohn Pedersen Fox, Murphy/Jahn, and Skidmore, Owings & Merrill still have a strong grip on the foreign markets, Britons such as Foster and Partners and Richard Rogers, and the Italian office of Renzo Piano Building Workshop, continue to erect imaginative technical and formal solutions for skyscrapers all over the world.[18] And more important, we see buildings such as the Taipei Financial Center, by C. Y. Lee & Partners, this year's world's tallest structure at 1,667 feet, nearing completion in Taipei. Back in 1996, K. Y. Cheung Design Associates erected Shun Hing Square, a tower 1,263 feet high, in Shenzhen, near Hong Kong. It is understandable why the desire to do something that could reassert America's hegemony vis-à-vis the skyscraper would overcome the fear of heights in replacing the World Trade Center towers.

With the impetus on creating high and mighty skyscrapers, the role of the engineer, working side by side with the architect, takes on a greater and greater visibility. Guy Nordenson's investigations of torqued towers is now all the more notable with the design of the Freedom Tower; but other engineers, such as Büro Happold, Arup, and Jörg Schlaich of Schlaich Bergermann und Partner, among others, contributed greatly to the various efforts of the teams working on the Innovative Design Study for the Lower Manhattan Development Corporation.

Many of the skyscraper projects shown in the following pages would require extremely adventurous engineers so that these structures can be made of flowing structural shapes that bend and twist toward the sky, and so their facades can change digitally from vibrant color to vibrant color in a flash, and so that these buildings can provide us with sources of extra energy instead of using it all up. And in many of the renderings there is the latent wish to be ever more invisible as we go higher. Is it possible to make a transparent skyscraper? Not yet, but it is easy enough to make it look as if it is disappearing into thin air through evanescent computer images.

Are we more cynical than optimistic to say that it is not likely that reality can approach the dreamy visions of computer imagery, especially when buildings appear as gossamery as spiderwebs? Back in 1973, Tafuri castigated architects for being too willing to "wander restlessly in the labyrinths of images" and be "enclosed in the stubborn silence of geometry content with its own perfection."[19]

Yes, Tafuri would spin in his grave if he knew about these concoctions. He would no doubt expect us, as do other critics, such as the philosopher Elizabeth Grosz, to be more suspicious of fantasies. Grosz contends that computerization and instant communications feed both the optimism and the anxiety in future-oriented thoughts. As she contended in a paper, "Future, Cities, Architecture," presented in 1996, "[Technology's] 'gift' to us is an increasing edginess about what the future holds in store, whether it promotes our every fantasy to the status of the attainable or the real, and whether we and our hopes are transformed beyond recognition into something other than what we are now."[20]

Grosz has a point. As much as we optimistically embrace the fantasies behind these visions, we should approach the process with a certain skepticism. Although the burst of the imaginary "what if" would enliven the rational landscape produced by politicians, developers, and civil engineers, and constantly determined by prevalent construction techniques and labor union practices, we cannot embrace the fantasies for their promise alone. Fantasies can be easily subverted. A gimlet eye must ascertain that the elixir being proffered is not just snake oil. These schemes brought to us by the well-meaning public officials, architects, and engineers offer many promises: buildings that disappear into the sky (Freedom Tower), a transportation hub that seems to hover above the sparkling white train platforms, a memorial where cool waters calm us on permanently sunny spring days. If this is reality, at least the other fantasies are advertised as what they are.

1. C. J. Blaauw, "Architectonisch Droomspiel," *Wendigen* 3 (1924), 3; quoted in Dennis Sharp, *Modern Architecture and Expressionism* (New York: George Braziller, 1966), 106.

2. Daniel J. Boorstin, *The Image: A Guide to Pseudo-Events in America* (New York: Atheneum, 1978), 183; originally published in 1962 as *The Image; or, What Happened to the American Dream*.

3. For Baudrillard's more Marxist and semiological analyses, see *Le Système des objets* (Paris: Gallimard, 1968), *La Société de consommation* (Paris: Gallimard, 1970), and *Simulacra and Simulations*, trans. Paul Foss, Paul Patton, and Philip Beitchman (New York: Sémiotext(e), 1983).

4. For a thorough history, see Sarah Bradford Landau and Carl Condit, *The Rise of the New York Skyscraper, 1865–1913* (New Haven: Yale University Press, 1996).

5. The term *skyscraper*, it should be noted, first appeared in a Chicago publication, "High Towers and Buildings," *Real Estate and Building Journal* (February 8, 1884), 364.

6. For more details, see David Rockefeller, *Memoirs* (New York: Random House, 2002).

7. For more details, see James Glanz and Eric Lipton, "The Height of Ambition," *New York Times Magazine* (September 8, 2002), 32–44, 59–60, 63; and *City in the Sky: The Rise and Fall of the World Trade Center* (New York: Times Books, 2004). Also see Robert A. M. Stern, Thomas Mellins, and David Fishman, *New York 1960* (New York: Monacelli Press, 1995), 198–206.

8. For an account of this effort in context of other plans for New York City at the time, see Suzanne Stephens, "A Fear of Filling," *Progressive Architecture* (June 1975), 48–57.

9. George Tamaro, "The World Trade Center 'Bathtub': From Genesis to Armegeddon," *The Bridge* (Spring 2002), 11–17.

10. Ada Louise Huxtable, "World Trade Center: Who's Afraid of the Big Bad Buildings?" *New York Times* (May 29, 1966), reprinted in Huxtable, *Will They Ever Finish Bruckner Boulevard?* (New York: Macmillan, 1970).

11. Ada Louise Huxtable, "Big But Not So Bold: The World Trade Center," *New York Times* (April 5, 1973), reprinted in Huxtable, *Kicked a Building Lately?* (New York: Quadrangle and New York Times Books, 1976), 122–23.

12. Gerald Allen, "The World Trade Center," *Architectural Record* (March 1974), 140–42.

13. Suzanne Stephens, "W.T.C. 2023," *Architectural Forum* (April 1973), 56–61.

14. Manfredo Tafuri, "The Disenchanted Mountain," in Giorgio Ciucci, Francesco Dal Co, Mario Manieri-Elia, and Manfredo Tafuri, *The American City: From the Civil War to the New Deal*, trans. Barbara Luigia La Penta (Cambridge, Mass.: MIT Press, 1979), 500.

15. For more details, see *The Lower Manhattan Plan: The 1966 Vision for Downtown New York*, ed. Carol Willis (reprint edition; New York: Princeton Architectural Press and the Skyscraper Museum, 2002).

16. Paul Willen and James Rossant, "In Retrospect," ibid., 31.

17. Adam Gopnik, "Higher and Higher, What Tall Buildings Do," *The New Yorker* (December 15, 2003), 112.

18. For more skyscrapers, see Eric Höweler, *Skyscraper: Vertical Now* (New York: Universe/Rizzoli, 2003).

19. Manfredo Tafuri, *Architecture and Utopia: Design and Capitalist Development*, trans. Barbara Luigia La Penta (Cambridge, Mass.: MIT Press, 1976), 181; Italian edition first published in 1973.

20. Elizabeth Grosz, *Architecture from the Outside: Essays on Virtual and Real Space* (Cambridge, Mass.: MIT Press, 2001), 50.

Official Proposals

Sponsored by the Lower Manhattan Development Corporation and the Port Authority of New York and New Jersey

The sickening loss of lives on September 11, 2001, at the World Trade Center, and at the Pentagon in Washington, D.C., and near Shanksville, Pennsylvania, was devastating for family members, friends, survivors, and those who observed the horrific events on television. The actual physical loss of the two World Trade Center towers themselves, completed in 1974 by Minoru Yamasaki and Emery Roth & Sons, was regretted by some, and not at all by others. As architecture, the 1,350-foot-high towers were best appreciated from far away as dramatically soaring markers on the New York City skyline. Up close, they were banal monoliths with faux-Gothic arches that ended abruptly at the ground in a mammoth windswept plaza.

Their destruction, along with the ruin and damage to surrounding buildings and the transportation infrastructure, has been crippling to New York's economy, not to mention the basic comfort of those working, living, and visiting downtown. But in urbanistic terms, the superblock on which the Twin Towers sat had done much to damage the interconnection between the various streets around the towers, isolating the area from the smaller-grained texture of lower Manhattan.

Now that reconstruction was needed, the opportunity presented itself to correct urbanistic problems. And there once again sprung the hope that Architecture with a capital A would have a chance to make a truly significant contribution to downtown, by creating new buildings, open spaces, and transportation facilities, along with a memorial to the victims.

But how to accomplish this? A constant complaint throughout the process of developing a master plan and a memorial for Ground Zero has been the lack of a real program and a real client. Maybe the problem was there were too many programs and too many clients with no clear lines of power, as the chart on page 28 indicates. The 16 acres on which the tower and the rest of the complex of buildings sat is owned by the Port Authority of New York and New Jersey, which is overseen by the two state governments. The Port Authority is not required to adhere to city zoning regulations, although it does encourage builders on its properties to adhere to local building codes. Shortly before the September 11 attacks, the Port Authority leased the 10 million square feet in the World Trade Center complex to private developer Larry Silverstein. He is obligated to pay $120 million in rent, and is proceeding with plans to build the first tower (Freedom Tower) on the site, in what can only be described as a squishily soft market, while he awaits settlement on an insurance claim. The insurance judgment will decide

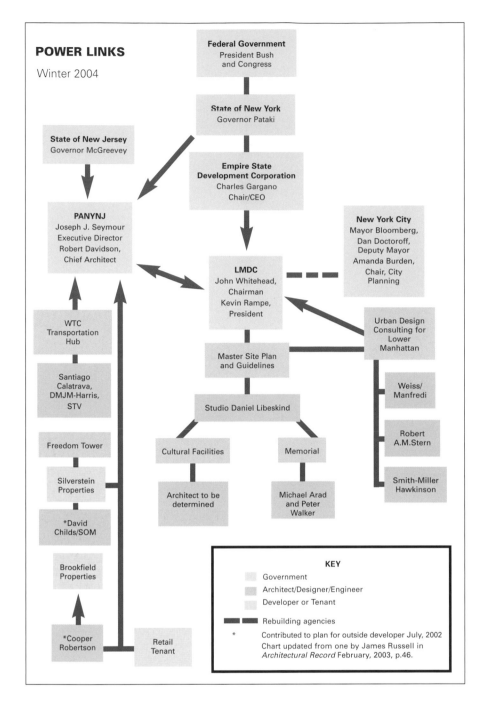

POWER LINKS

Winter 2004

Federal Government
President Bush
and Congress

State of New York
Governor Pataki

State of New Jersey
Governor McGreevey

**Empire State
Development Corporation**
Charles Gargano
Chair/CEO

New York City
Mayor Bloomberg,
Dan Doctoroff,
Deputy Mayor
Amanda Burden,
Chair, City
Planning

PANYNJ
Joseph J. Seymour
Executive Director
Robert Davidson,
Chief Architect

LMDC
John Whitehead,
Chairman
Kevin Rampe,
President

**Urban Design
Consulting for
Lower
Manhattan**

**WTC
Transportation
Hub**

**Master Site Plan
and Guidelines**

**Weiss/
Manfredi**

**Santiago
Calatrava,
DMJM-Harris,
STV**

Studio Daniel Libeskind

**Robert
A.M.Stern**

Freedom Tower

Cultural Facilities

Memorial

**Smith-Miller
Hawkinson**

**Silverstein
Properties**

**Architect to be
determined**

**Michael Arad
and Peter
Walker**

***David
Childs/SOM**

**Brookfield
Properties**

KEY

Government

Architect/Designer/Engineer

Developer or Tenant

Rebuilding agencies

*   Contributed to plan for outside developer July, 2002
Chart updated from one by James Russell in
Architectural Record February, 2003, p.46.

***Cooper
Robertson**

**Retail
Tenant**

money is funneled by Pataki through the Empire State Development Corporation, it is easy to say the reins of power clearly belong to the governor. But even Pataki has had to cede some control to Larry Silverstein.

As a landowner, the Port Authority needs income from the leases to pay off the bonds. Accordingly it must find a lessee for at least 600,000 square feet of retail space. Before the attacks, Westfield America had signed on; but since then the lease has been returned to the Port Authority, with Westfield getting a cash settlement of $140 million. This is considered good news by the planning community, since Westfield had made known its plan to keep retail space below ground on the concourse connecting to transit. Westfield strongly objected to placing retail at street level, seen by planners as an opportunity to enhance pedestrian activity in the area. In addition, the lease for the destroyed twenty-four-story Marriott Hotel (formerly Vista International) at 3 World Trade Center was term inated with the Port Authority. The deal requires Marriott to pay the balance for the cost of the Skidmore, Owings & Merrill–designed hotel, which Marriott bought in 1995, but also allows Marriott to collect insurance benefits.

whether Silverstein is compensated $7 billion, the price placed on the destruction of both towers as separate occurrences, or $3.5 billion, if the two towers are treated as one occurrence. If it is one occurrence, Silverstein may decide to take a reduced reimbursement and depart the scene. Then the Port Authority would seek another developer, who might hire another architect. In the meantime, Silverstein is proceeding with the unencumbered construction of 7 World Trade Center, designed by David Childs and Skidmore, Owings & Merrill on the north edge of the site.

In the months following the destruction of September 11, the Lower Manhattan Development Corporation (LMDC) was formed as a subsidiary of the Empire State Development Corporation, which is controlled by New York State Governor George Pataki. LMDC would work with the Port Authority in planning the area. Although New York City's Mayor Michael Bloomberg selected half of the LMDC board, the city has no official role in the planning process. Meanwhile, the other half of the board was selected by Pataki. Since the then-promised $21 billion in federal

At one point in the tangled process, right after Studio Daniel Libeskind was selected as the master planner for the site, it looked as if the Port Authority was going to swap the WTC land with New York City, plus kick in $500 to $700 million in return for LaGuardia and Kennedy airports, which are only leased by the Port Authority. The city wanted to keep some sort of control over the airports, however, and the idea seemed to die from over-deliberated negotiations.

The specific process for reconstructing Ground Zero has turned out to be a thorny and complicated one. Needed right away was a master plan, with urban design guidelines, for which Beyer Blinder Belle and engineers Parsons Brinkerhoff were selected on May 22, 2002. But after a public rejection of the schemes (more about that later), the LMDC and the Port Authority staged a competition for an "Innovative Design Study." Seven teams had presented nine schemes on December 18, 2002. Of those, Studio Daniel Libeskind with his "Memory Foundations" and the THINK team with its "World Cultural Center" were named

Site plan, World Trade Center site
before September 11, 2001, with
gray figures denoting buildings in
WTC complex

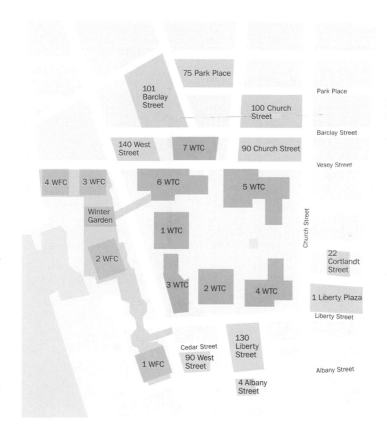

as finalists on February 4, 2003. Then Libeskind was designated the "designer for the redevelopment for the World Trade Center site plan" (as New Jersey Governor James McGreevey called it) by the LMDC and the Port Authority on February 27, 2003.

Another major issue confronting the LMDC and the Port Authority involved the creation of a memorial within the actual precinct of the former World Trade Center complex. A separate competition was held for the memorial in summer 2003. Of that open competition, which attracted artists, architects, and designers, architect Michael Arad and landscape architect Peter Walker were selected as a team on January 6, 2004.

The first major structure to go up on the site is the aforementioned Freedom Tower being developed by Larry Silverstein, with David Childs of Skidmore, Owings & Merrill as the design architect and project manager, and Libeskind the collaborating architect during concept and schematic design phases. The result of this difficult marriage of two designers was unveiled on December 19, 2003.

Earlier in the year (July 31, 2003), the Port Authority, on its own, announced that Santiago Calatrava, the Spanish-born engineer and architect, would design the World Trade Center Transportation Hub. Calatrava, as part of the Downtown Design Partnership, would be working in a joint venture with DMJM + Harris and STV Group, with the understanding that he would follow the guidelines set up by Libeskind. That scheme was unveiled with great fanfare on January 22, 2004.

It is still unclear how much of Daniel Libeskind's vision will remain intact as these first three components—the Freedom Tower, the memorial, and the WTC Transportation Hub—go forward. Much of the problem could be attributed to the unresolved issues about the difference between architectural image and the master plan, as architect Rafael Viñoly noted in an op-ed piece in the New York Times, December 12, 2003: "The planner decides where buildings go, how big they are, the kind of urban form they create and the purposes they serve. A planner marks out roads and figures out how the underground infrastructure relates to the surface infrastructure. What a master planner does not do is design the buildings themselves." During the whole process Libeskind's "vision," in Viñoly's words (or you could say "image"), involving a sunken memorial site and a spiraling array of towers, ending in the 1,776-foot-high spire, won over Governor Pataki and a good part of the public. The detail Libeskind gave his scheme was perceived as a "design guide-line" for carrying out the master plan. Viñoly attributes the public misapprehension about the extent of Libeskind's involvement in the design to the LMDC's reluctance to clarify the difference between the master plan and the architecture. Why did they do this? As Viñoly astutely points out, when Beyer Blinder Belle presented its master planning schemes in July 2002, it showed schematic building blocks in place of architectural designs.

The public—and most of the press—decided what you see is what you get. And they roundly repudiated the master plans. This is what led to the second round, or the "Innovative Design Study," in which seven teams presented master plans in December 2002. Even though the winner of the Innovative Design Study competition was simply supposed to be a consultant to the agency on developing the master plan, the story had already been rewritten in the public mind. The winner was both the master planner and architect. LMDC did not try to alter that impression. There was too much enthusiasm, too much public interest.

As the process bumps along, more transformation and modification is bound to occur in the ten to fifteen years it takes to rebuild the complex. Already some of the officials running the show at the LMDC have changed. John Whitehead, chairman of the LMDC, is still in charge; but Louis Tomson has been succeeded by Kevin Rampe as president, and Alexander Garvin, initially vice president for planning, design, and development, has been succeeded by Andrew Winters (now called vice president and director of planning, design, and development). Affecting the redevelopment, of course, is the economic question: Who foots the bill? The price tag for rebuilding the World Trade Center site was estimated to be about $10 billion in May 2003. Yet the LMDC has said that private money would be required for some of the cultural buildings, and particularly for the $350-million memorial. The finances may alter the picture severely.

Before we begin to move backward in time over the events of the last few years, we should clarify where we are now, at the beginning of 2004. Much has yet to be determined: The designs for three major components—Freedom Tower, the memorial, and the World Trade Center Transportation Hub—have recently been made public, but their designs could change at a future date. It has happened before.

The court case for the insurance claim by Larry Silverstein, the private developer who is building Freedom Tower, is still going on. The guidelines to the master plan for the World Trade Center site that Studio Daniel Libeskind is working up for the Lower Manhattan Development Corporation and the Port Authority of New York and New Jersey are expected any day (or month) now. That situation is also unpredictable. Certainly the look of the master plan has changed since Libeskind was selected as the presumed master planner in February 2003.

The LMDC report on the creation of a "cultural district," the next stage of the rebuilding process, was released February 10, 2004. It outlines not only the creation of a Memorial Center below ground as part of Michael Arad and Peter Walker's design for the memorial, but proposes locations for buildings above grade. A performing arts center, about 100,000 to 200,000 square feet in size, is planned for the intersection of Greenwich and Fulton streets, east of the site of the Freedom Tower. Just south of this building more cultural facilities are being developed by the LMDC in consultation with Studio Daniel Libeskind: placed to the west of the WTC Transportation Hub (aka PATH Transit Hall), they would supply about 200,000 to 250,000 square feet for several museums and cultural institutions. In the next few months the actual cultural institutions that have expressed interest in moving to the site may be chosen, and, at some future date, an architect named. Will Libeskind get to design a building? That too remains to be seen.

Meanwhile the LMDC is embroiled with preservationists in a controversy about the extent that the ruins and traces of the World Trade Center structures will be kept for public access. According to law, sites receiving federal money must be reviewed for their eligibility for listing on the National Register of Historic Places. The LMDC and preservationists both agree that the Ground Zero site should be eligible, but they are at loggerheads about whether the rebuilding process would have an adverse affect on the features of the site that are now considered historic: the slurry wall in the concrete bathtub, the remnants of column footings, plus a cast-iron tube that belonged to the Hudson & Manhattan Railroad.

Courtesy of the *New York Times*; illustrations by Mika Grondahl. (Sources: Studio Daniel Libeskind; Skidmore, Owings & Merrill)

Evolution of a Tower

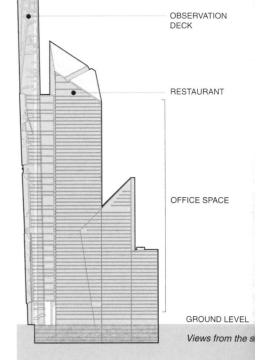

DECEMBER 2002

Studio Daniel Libeskind s original proposa a 1,776-foot skyscraper at the World Trade Center site was called Vertical World Gardens. The almost freestanding spire w to be filled in its upper reaches with trees plants. Offices would have reached the 64 floor.

The scale of these drawings relative to one another is approximate.

OBSERVATION DECK

RESTAURANT

OFFICE SPACE

GROUND LEVEL

Views from the s

The tube and various artifacts at the hangar at Kennedy International Airport could go into the memorial museum, but how much is shown of the slurry wall and traces of the column footings needs to be sorted out. The Coalition of 9/11 Families is pursuing the matter through governmental representatives and lawyers, bolstering the complaints from the New York Landmarks Conservancy and the Historic Districts Council, among others, that the process is proceeding too quickly.

Shown on these pages is a series of drawings, printed in the *New York Times*, December 26, 2002, which illustrate the transmogrifications Daniel Libeskind's vision for the World Trade Center site's highest tower is taking on its way to being realized by David Childs of SOM and the developer Larry Silverstein. Also shown is the site plan for the current World Trade Center area. Like the tower, this too has gone through changes since Libeskind's winning scheme was announced on February 27, 2003. What is interesting to note is how similar the land-use pattern is to the original Beyer Blinder Belle schemes of 2002, and to a scheme Cooper Robertson executed for neighboring landholder Brookfield Financial Properties.

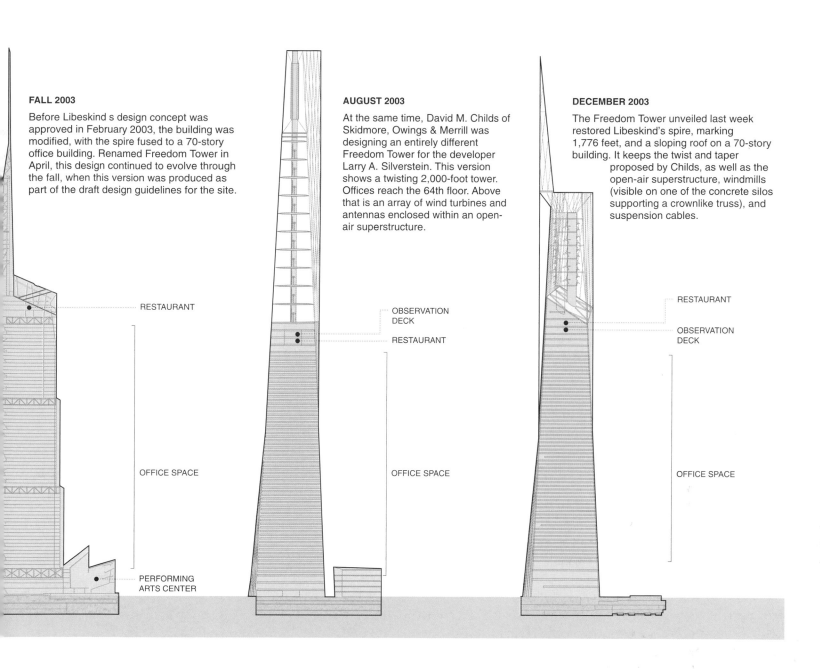

FALL 2003

Before Libeskind's design concept was approved in February 2003, the building was modified, with the spire fused to a 70-story office building. Renamed Freedom Tower in April, this design continued to evolve through the fall, when this version was produced as part of the draft design guidelines for the site.

RESTAURANT

OFFICE SPACE

PERFORMING ARTS CENTER

AUGUST 2003

At the same time, David M. Childs of Skidmore, Owings & Merrill was designing an entirely different Freedom Tower for the developer Larry A. Silverstein. This version shows a twisting 2,000-foot tower. Offices reach the 64th floor. Above that is an array of wind turbines and antennas enclosed within an open-air superstructure.

OBSERVATION DECK

RESTAURANT

OFFICE SPACE

DECEMBER 2003

The Freedom Tower unveiled last week restored Libeskind's spire, marking 1,776 feet, and a sloping roof on a 70-story building. It keeps the twist and taper proposed by Childs, as well as the open-air superstructure, windmills (visible on one of the concrete silos supporting a crownlike truss), and suspension cables.

RESTAURANT

OBSERVATION DECK

OFFICE SPACE

Libeskind's vision for the site, first revealed on December 18, 2002, then modified by February 27, 2003 (when he was selected winner), and further revised September 17, 2003, is proving highly vulnerable to reality. What remains is that typical response to dreams and fantasies: compromise.

Other matters of note: New York City government has stayed discreetly at the side while the lines are drawn in the sand. Yet just recently, as David Dunlap noted in the *New York Times* on March 2, 2004, the City Planning department, headed by Amanda Burden, was "breaking its conspicuous public silence on the World Trade Center redevelopment plan" by advocating the return of more city streets to the site. It wants to see Dey and Courtlandt streets brought back to activate the area. (They sometimes appear and disappear from LMDC drawings.) On top of that, according to Deputy Mayor Daniel Doctoroff, the city owns the streets—and former streets—of the WTC site, adding up to approximately 2.5 acres of land. With the demolition of the Deutsche Bank building south of Liberty Street providing more open space to the LMDC, a matter that was only decided recently, it does seem as if the ground underneath us shifts as we walk and talk.

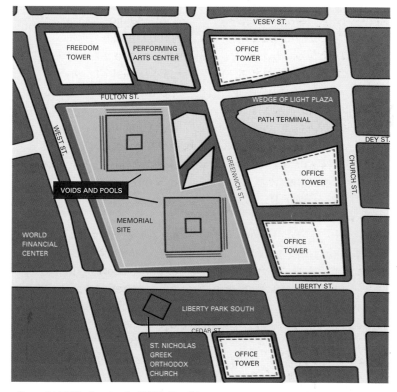

Current LMDC site plan for WTC site; this version without Dey and Courtlandt streets

Freedom Tower

December 19, 2003

David Childs, Skidmore, Owings & Merrill, design architect and project manager

Daniel Libeskind, collaborating architect during concept and schematic design phases

ABOVE View from south toward Freedom Tower surrounded by possible towers to the east and south

OPPOSITE Computer image of Freedom Tower from the Hudson River

Image clashed with reality in the summer of 2003, over and over and over. Image was represented by Daniel Libeskind's spiraling 1,776-foot-high tower with its off-center spire, which captivated New York State Governor George Pataki enough for him to select Libeskind's scheme as the master plan for the site in February 2003. Reality came in the form of Larry Silverstein, who has the lease for the 10-million-square-foot commercial space once part of the World Trade Center. His architect, David Childs of Skidmore, Owings & Merrill, did not quite agree with Libeskind's vision, and so the two duked it out over the summer and fall. Since Childs, with SOM, is called the design architect and project manager, and Libeskind the collaborating architect during concept and schematic design phases, it is amazing that the building doesn't look more like a camel by committee. (Governor Pataki backed Libeskind to the end, and insisted the two come to terms on a scheme.)

Perhaps everyone's expectations had been so lowered by the stories of strife between Childs and Libeskind that the presentation on December 19, 2003, came as a pleasant surprise. The reaction was polite, even nice, with such generally heard observations as "it could be a little more resolved." Although some observers in the architectural community agreed that Libeskind's spire now looked like a prosthetic device welded at the last minute to Child's tower, few complained loudly. (Even Childs admitted at the time that the spire was not properly integrated yet, and needed to be worked out.) If New York critics seemed happy with the scheme, out-of-towners were less euphoric. Nicolai Ouroussoff of the *Los Angeles Times* wrote that "what is most striking about the design … is its lack of originality" and called it "diluted" and only "slightly better-than-average."

The Freedom Tower, located on the northwest corner of the site, is bulkier and less angled than Libeskind's original 1,776-foot-high tower. Its torqued and tapered body offers 2.6 million square feet of office space (up to the fifty-eighth floor), with mechanical floors

above, and an observation deck, event space, and a restaurant on the sixty-sixth, sixty-seventh, and sixty-eighth floors. Another observation deck is located at a 1,400-foot height in the top of the tower, where an open-air light steel structure of cables and trusses will house wind-harvesting turbines. Conceived to take advantage of the strong prevailing winds off the Hudson and East Rivers, the turbines are promised to provide 20 percent of the building's power. Finally, above this top portion, at 1,500 feet, the 276-foot spire brings the total height to 1,776 feet.

Childs worked out the design with engineer Guy Nordenson so that a diagonal structural grid of steel encloses the tower. Combined with an interior concrete core, the tower, with its torqued or twisting form, maintains its stability against wind and gravity as it tapers. Additional safety features are provided by extra-strong fireproofing and biological and chemical filters for air supply. David Childs asserts certain concerns are being subjected to ongoing scrutiny (including fears of migrating birds being drawn into the wind turbines, noise from the turbines, and

other environmental considerations). The tower, estimated to cost $1.5 billion, is clad in glass (blast resistant at the lobby level) that will be energy-efficient in terms of heat gain and loss. Retail space is placed underground in a concourse that links to transportation nodes. Although the tower is expected to take five years to build, it might take longer to fill up, owing to the very sluggish real estate market in this area.

Regardless of how light, airy, and evanescent the computerized renderings of the project

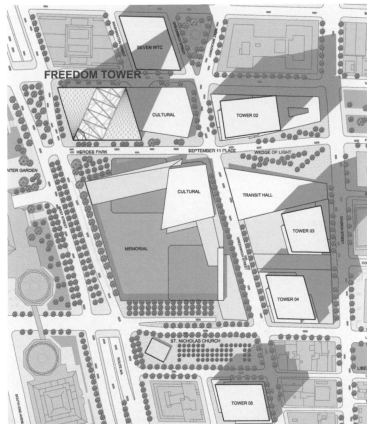

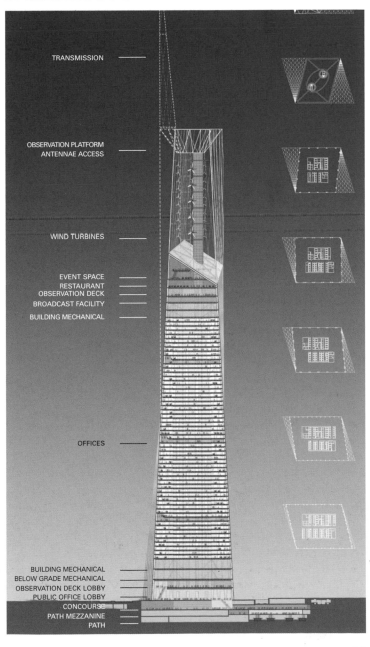

show it to be, the building in reality may not easily approach an all-that's-solid-melts-into-the-air transparency. Even the white glass shown now could end up being cheaper and darker by the end of construction. And the top third of the open frame will have so much going on (cables, windmills, elevator cores, steel structure) that it can't appear to be the delicate spiderweb it looks like in renderings. But SOM learned one important thing: how to render bulk to appear almost invisible.

Memorial Competition

November 19, 2003–January 14, 2004

ABOVE Winning scheme by Michael Arad and Peter Walker, announced January 14, 2004. View of memorial plaza from southwest (model: Awad Architectural Models)

OPPOSITE View from the southeast

A memorial to the victims of the terrorist attacks has been a significant and distinct component of the rebuilding process, encouraged by the commitment of groups representing families of the victims. Included among those to be memorialized are not only the 2,749 victims of September 11, 2001, in New York (revised as of January 2004), but also the 184 in the Pentagon and 40 from the crash near Shanksville, Pennsylvania, and the six who died in the previous World Trade Center bombing on February 26, 1993.

For the memorial space, 4.7 acres around and including the footprints of the tower, the LMDC decided to stage an open competition. An outside jury of thirteen reviewed the submissions, including three design professionals—Maya Lin, famous for her Vietnam Veterans Memorial in Washington, D.C.; Enrique Norten of TEN Arquitectos in Mexico, who is designing the Brooklyn Public Library's Visual and Performing Arts Library, plus a mixed-use office tower in Harlem; and Michael Van Valkenburgh, a landscape architect and professor at the Harvard Design School. The participants in the competition were given certain guidelines, such as: to abide by the distinct boundaries within the site defined by Fulton, Greenwich, West, and Liberty streets; to make the footprints of the towers visible; to leave the slurry wall exposed; to enable visitors to get to bedrock; and to list the names of the victims. The competition drew 5,201 entries from sixty-three countries.

Eight finalists, many of whom were young architects and artists, were announced on November 19, 2003. By January 6, 2004, Michael Arad, an architect for the New York City Housing Authority, who teamed up with landscape architect Peter Walker of Berkeley, California, was selected the winner, and his design, "Reflecting Absence," was presented publicly on January 14. Arad had brought in Walker after the finalists were announced in November. The coupling apparently was a stratagem encouraged by the LMDC and its jurors, who seemed to take to heart the oft-heard comment during the exhibition of the finalists' schemes that "Reflecting Absence" was stark.

The public reaction to the eight finalists' schemes was not overwhelmingly enthusiastic. In fact, many observers and critics expressed downright disappointment. The schemes appeared too similar, emphasizing waterfalls and reflecting pools, beams of light, long planar walls with names carved in them (à la Maya Lin's Vietnam Veterans Memorial). General comments pointed to the projects' abstractness, their funereal quality, and their minimalist aesthetic. Many of the schemes' accompanying explanations showed a desire to turn the abstract elements into heavy-handed symbols of grief (water representing tears; beams of light for stars and victims' souls; a translucent, perhaps skid-inducing plaza becoming a "bandage healing a wound"). The impracticality of many of the finalists' schemes was also evident: for example, acres of water in an icy, windy climate; lamps lighted by liquid fuel underground; a translucent surface extending across the plaza. While many critics did not support having figurative schemes (statues of heroes) or other such traditional memorial approaches, two factors seemed to cause discontent: the process itself, and the pressure to do something now. Michael Kimmelman, art critic for the *New York Times*, urged in an essay, December 7, 2003, that the LMDC "forget the vapid populism" of the open competition, and limit the selection process. He also suggested allowing more time to come up with a scheme. As *Architectural Record*'s editor in chief Robert Ivy stated in his editorial in the January 2004 issue, "The best advice is to slow down, allow time to pass and our perspective to clear, and then to build." This did not happen. Again and again, an old refrain sounded: New York's Governor Pataki wanted ground broken for the memorial by fall 2004.

Just before the winning scheme, "Reflecting Absence," was announced, the jury was reported to be favoring "Garden of Lights" by Pierre David with Sean Corriel and Jessica Kmetovic, and "Passages of Light: The Memorial Cloud" by Gisela Baurmann, Sawad Brooks, and Jonas Coersmeier. Arad's scheme was also considered a strong contender, but his selection depended on making substantive changes to address LMDC reservations. The lack of access to the perimeter column footings at the bottom of the former towers' foundations was a concern, along with Arad's specifying eastern pine trees, which are vulnerable to pollution and high winds, and his inclusion of a new structure for cultural purposes along the west side.

Michael Arad and Peter Walker
Reflecting Absence

ABOVE Stairs at Liberty Street

OPPOSITE View of family memorial room (**TOP**) and view of memorial gallery (**BOTTOM**)

By the time Arad and Walker's revised winning scheme was revealed in January 2004, it had been softened with many more trees—deciduous, not pine—and pavers and low ground cover on the plaza level. Arad's new west building for cultural purposes had disappeared. But the 200-foot-square voids remained, demarcating the footprints of the tower, with sheets of water cascading 30 feet into gigantic reflecting pools, and then, in the center, falling another 15 feet into smaller square pools. Steps lead up to the plaza where the grade changed, so that parts of the plaza are now elevated above the sidewalk. A more developed nether region was appar-

ent below ground. A ramp next to the north tower's footprint/void would lead down past the exposed parts of the slurry wall to a 30-foot-high, 65,000-square-foot underground museum space to contain artifacts (fire engines, pieces of the building) placed beneath the southwest plaza. (Another ramp occurs on the southeast corner.) In the north tower void, at bedrock 70 feet below ground, sits a container—much like a giant sarcophagus—for the unidentified remains of the victims.

The reaction to the scheme was polite and in some cases congratulatory. Questions and

doubts remained for the more skeptical critics. The elevation of the plaza would make it psychologically more inaccessible to the general public, much like the plazas along the high-rise towers on Avenue of the Americas in Midtown, once devoid of people until the food vendors camped out along the edges. The site of the plaza with two voids reminded many of the large and maligned windswept one that existed there before. Although this would be planted with trees, they would be bare five months a year.

Below ground, the spaces look like an underground parking garage. If poured-in-place concrete is used, it is wise to keep in mind that superb concrete construction is not something New York City is known for—unlike Japan, where concrete may be poured into lacquered wood forms. The best surface would be expensive stone or marble cladding, but already officials claim they have to raise an estimated $350 million privately for the cost of the memorial.

The presence of so much water has raised more questions. Fountains and pools bring psychological relief in a hot, arid climate. But they are not so pleasant in a location with high winds and freezing temperatures. The National Park Service, which would be in charge of maintenance, generally turns off the fountains in the winter, which in this case leaves a lot of empty pool bottoms exposed to view.

And if water were indeed running, Arad has stated that glass would not separate the visitors underground from the spray of the cascading water, another discomfiting factor. Such underground spaces also would be extremely dreary if the lighting were low-maintenance (and cheap) fluorescent illumination. Extremely sophisticated (and expensive) lighting would be necessary to create the suitably spiritual atmosphere. In addition to all this, questions of security in a once targeted area remain to be addressed. Such practical issues may be confronted now that Davis Brody Bond has been named associate architect.

FINALISTS

November 19, 2003

Michael Arad

New York City

Reflecting Absence (initial proposal)

Prior to Peter Walker's participation,
Michael Arad submitted this proposal.
Reflecting pools cover the footprints of the
World Trade Center towers in voids that drop
to 30 feet below grade. At street level the
voids are surrounded by a plaza, originally
to be planted with pine trees, while an angu-
lar structure for cultural uses along West
Street has been added by Arad to buffer the
memorial from the noise of traffic.

bbc art + architecture— Gisela Baurmann, Sawad Brooks, and Jonas Coersmeier

New York City

Passages of Light: The Memorial Cloud

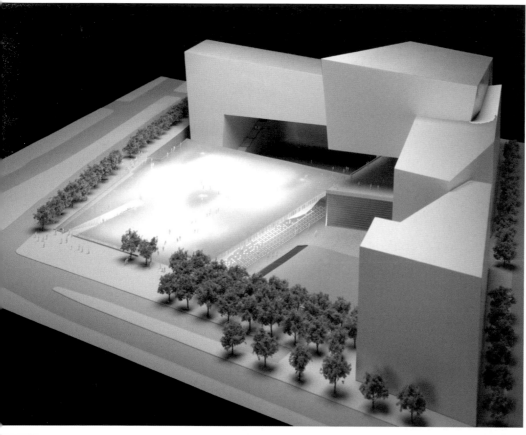

At street level, the open space is covered by a translucent surface (left), the top of a "cloud" formed from 10,000 vertical conduits for light. This cloud would hang over an underground level (below, right), where victims' names would be engraved within circles of light (below, left).

Pierre David
with Sean Corriel and
Jessica Kmetovic

Paris, France

Garden of Lights

This three-level scheme features two "prairies" of vegetation covering the footprints of the former towers on the top level (model, view from south, left, and view from north, below, right). Between them is an orchard. On the middle level are two rooms the size of the footprints. The south room is filled with light; the north room features a wall made from steel salvaged from the towers. On the other side of this wall are 1,275 lights (one for each physically unidentified victim). A passage, edged with a stream and lined with roses, connects the two rooms (below, left). On the lowest level is a room of 2,982 cylindrical alabaster altars, on which shine a constellation of starlike lights.

Bradley Campbell and Matthias Neumann

New York City

Lower Waters

A black granite-clad memorial building is located on the north footprint (left), with a private area for the victims' families as well as a public area. A waterfall and a pool is integrated into this structure (below. right), while the south footprint is devoted to a grove of trees. Underground, in the space between the two footprints, is a Museum of September 11, from which visitors could see the slurry wall. The facade of this museum, which is in the footprint of the south tower, is stacked glass with sanded edges. A wall surrounding the entire site (below, left) is inscribed with the victims' names.

Toshio Sasaki

New York City

Inversion of Light

A street-level bermed park surrounds the footprints (right and below). The one belonging to the north tower has the floor plan of the ninety-fourth and ninety-fifth floors reproduced on its surface, and is illuminated from underneath. The footprint of the south tower is covered by a reflecting pool, also illuminated from underneath. Underground, the north glass wall of the memorial is etched with the victims' names, with water trickling down behind the glass (bottom). The unidentified remains of the victims are enclosed by two semicircular glass walls, topped with a circular skylight.

Brian Strawn and Karla Sierralta

Chicago, Illinois

Dual Memory

The footprint of the south tower contains sugar maple trees on a plinth (right), which edge a depressed open space enclosed by stone walls with memorial messages (below). The footprint of the north tower is occupied by a pavilion whose roof is punctured with light portals, one for each victim, illuminating a below-ground gallery (bottom) where images and biographies of the victims would be installed.

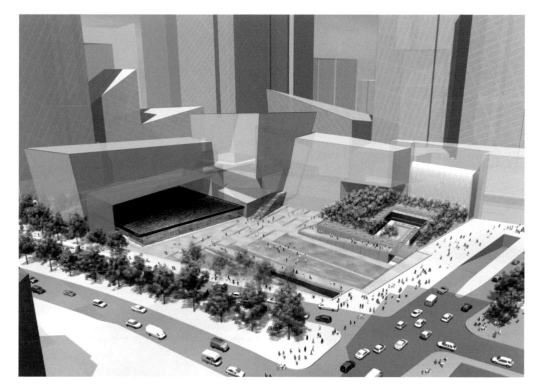

Norman Lee and Michael Lewis

Houston, Texas

Votives in Suspension

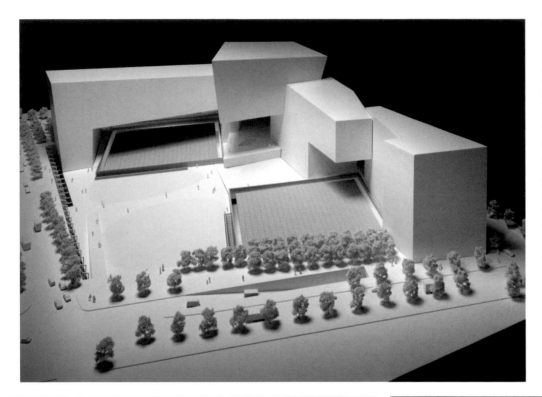

Two below-ground sanctuaries in the footprints of the World Trade Center towers have votive lights (one for each victim) suspended by cables above reflecting pools (below, right). Liquid fuel containers in the cables keep the votive flames going. Narrow slots edging the footprints admit natural light down into the interior, and the perimeter wall of the memorial sanctuary (below, left) lists the names of the victims. At street level, parapet walls demarcate the footprints of the original towers (left), with the slurry wall exposed on the west. On the southern side of the park is a "Liberty Wall," on which is engraved a historical time line of the site.

Joseph Karadin
with Hsin-Yi Wu

New York City

Suspending Memory

At street level two gardens on the footprints of the towers contain, along with trees, concrete and glass columns—one for each victim (below, right). The two garden-islands are separated by water covering almost the whole site (left), with the two linked by a commemorative bridge. In the north garden, a natural stone wall is inlaid with randomly placed, polished squares representing the victims (below, left). Water trickles from the base of each square into a "Pool of Tears."

World Trade Center Transportation Hub

January 22, 2004

Downtown Design Partnership: Santiago Calatrava, DMJM + Harris, and STV Group

ABOVE WTC Transportation Hub, mezzanine level (ticketing)

OPPOSITE, BOTTOM View east from across Greenwich Street

OPPOSITE, TOP Model showing wings extended (left) and closed (right)

The World Trade Center Transportation Hub burst upon the scene in late January 2004 with little prelude. In one fell swoop it stole the thunder from the hoopla surrounding the memorial designed by Michael Arad and Peter Walker, and the Freedom Tower that David Childs of Skidmore, Owings & Merrill is executing (with Daniel Libeskind as collaborating architect) for developer Larry Silverstein.

It is ironic that the most seductive piece to arrive in this triplet of new components at the World Trade Center site is the progeny solely of the Port Authority of New York and New Jersey. Long considered to be architecturally challenged, the Port Authority has for the past two years been partnering with the LMDC to produce a master plan, guidelines, and key architectural components for the site. And what happens? The Port Authority

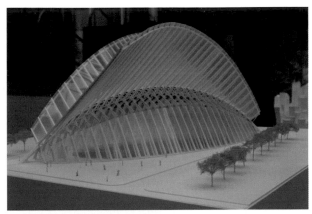

grabs the limelight by giving birth to this light steel-and-glass-winged creature all by itself.

The Port Authority had already been burnishing its architectural image with a well-regarded temporary station designed by its chief architect, Robert Davidson. And it made no secret that it would select the architect and engineers for this PATH (Port Authority Trans-Hudson) station, with its links to subways and ferries. But the process behind the selection of Santiago Calatrava, DMJM + Harris, and STV Group was hardly made public, or, to use the new catch word, "transparent." Indeed, six weeks before the announcement of Calatrava's appointment, the site's master planner, Daniel Libeskind, had a letter of intent from the Port Authority that he would design the main transit hall (at least according to the *New York Times*, June 19, 2003). Previously the Port Authority had sent out Requests for Qualifications to a series of firms with experience in transportation and engineering. The shortlist included three teams: engineers Parsons Brinkerhoff/URS and architect William Pedersen of Kohn Pedersen Fox; engineers The Washington Group with architect Rafael Viñoly; and Calatrava, who had been

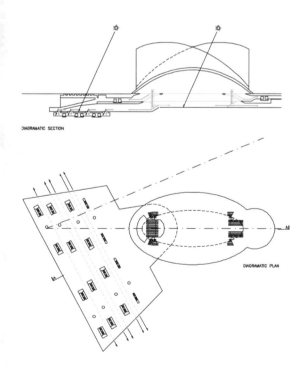

DIAGRAMATIC SECTION

DIAGRAMATIC PLAN

approached by DMJM + Harris and STV Group. The Spanish-born architect and engineer, famous for sculptural airports, transit stations, and bridges, won wide acclaim for his Milwaukee Art Museum and the Tenerife Auditorium in Santa Cruz, Canary Islands.

The Calatrava-designed transportation hub will occupy a parcel of land edged by Fulton, Greenwich, Church, and Dey streets. This means that a good portion of the "Wedge of Light" plaza so integral to Daniel Libeskind's winning master plan of February 2003 has been usurped by the hub. (Libeskind claims this is not a problem.) The arched oval form, with its steel ribbed canopy wings, is perched on a concrete substructure. The oval structure comprises two 300-foot-long parallel steel arches that rise along the ridge of the roof to a height of 96 feet. The operable canopy is constructed of L-shaped steel frames that ride on each of the steel ribs and cantilever to a height of 150 feet above the roof. A tension ring at ground level and a compression ring 22 feet below grade at the upper concourse level keep the rib cage stable. During temperate weather, the Port Authority says, the two wings can open to a 50-foot width at the center. Meanwhile, glass adhering to environmental standards is still

to be determined, and the design has to undergo wind tunnel tests.

Commuters entering the transit hub will descend 22 feet to the large oval space of the upper concourse. From there they take elevators and stairs to the main (lower) concourse level another 20 feet below ground. And then they descend another 14 feet to the mezzanine level for ticketing, and finally another 14 feet to the train platforms. This space, about 70 feet below the street, receives natural light through glass block floors. The natural light entering the hub should be amplified by the use of a light surface material, which is to be chosen later.

To be sure, the material for floors and walls will have to retain its whiteness in spite of 80,000 commuters and New York City dirt if the interior is to retain the drama of the renderings, which failed to show the signage, kiosks, and retail outlets that generally clutter transit hubs. And money is a consideration: the hub is expected to cost more than Freedom Tower. The price is $2 billion with $1.7 billion donated by the Federal Transit Administration. And then comes maintenance. Some wonder what time reality pulls in to the station.

Innovative Design Study

Competition for Master Site Plan

December 18, 2002–September 17, 2003

ABOVE Daniel Libeskind

RIGHT Rafael Viñoly of THINK

BELOW, LEFT Norman Foster

BELOW, RIGHT Roger Duffy of Skidmore, Owings & Merrill

The period between December 2002 and September 2003 was significant for the development of the World Trade Center site. On December 18, 2002, the finalists for the LMDC-sponsored Innovative Design Study presented their schemes. By February 4, 2003, two contenders remained in the running to design the master plan. By February 27, 2003, the winner was announced: Studio Daniel Libeskind, who continued to work on their winning scheme throughout the ensuing months. Libeskind's refined master plan was finally revealed on September 17, 2003, and for a brief period architecture had become a spectator sport.

The media overdrive in covering the presentation of nine schemes by seven architecture and urban design teams on December 18, 2002, came as a gratifying surprise to the architecture community. Some of the best-known talents were represented on the teams, such as Norman Foster, Richard Meier, Peter Eisenman, Charles Gwathmey, Steven Holl, Rafael Viñoly, and Libeskind, along with a slew of up-and-coming firms, such as Greg Lynn, Foreign Office Architects, UN Studio, and Michael Maltzan. The architects came from London, Tokyo, Los Angeles, Amsterdam, not to mention New York. Would this heady mix actually affect what was going to happen at Ground Zero? That no one could answer, but the array of ideas and visions seen that day were to give the press and the public much to debate.

After the July 20, 2002, Town Hall meeting at the Javits Center, in which schemes by architects Beyer Blinder Belle were trounced by the public for being uninspiring, the LMDC sent out a Request for Qualifications (RFQ) in August. The deadline was September 16. Even though the ultimate winner, Libeskind, was treated by the press (and the LMDC) as potential master planner for the site, the RFQ included this disclaimer: "This is NOT a design competition and will not result in the selection of a final plan. It is intended to generate creative and varied concepts to help plan the future of the site." The LMDC also let it be known that it would seek the counsel of New York New Visions, a pro bono coalition of twenty-one architecture, engineering, planning, landscape architecture, and other design organizations, in the selection of the teams.

From the 406 submissions of credentials received, the LMDC and the Port Authority selected six teams of architects and planners and various other consultants in late September 2002. The LMDC added one more team, in-house consultants Peterson/Littenberg Architecture and Urban Design. The seven

competitors had two months (with periodic review with the LMDC) to develop their proposals. For their efforts they were given $40,000, a woefully small sum for the number of hours their various offices would devote. But they were also given more programmatic flexibility than Beyer Blinder Belle in coming up with a master plan: the new program called for 6.5 million to 10 million square feet of office space, instead of the 11 million asked of Beyer Blinder Belle. Yet the retail square footage was expanded from 600,000 to one million square feet. In addition to cultural amenities, the program called for a "powerful skyline element" as part of the plan, and encouraged residential components to be included near the site (the Port Authority claims it has no jurisdiction for residential uses on the land it owns). The LMDC program also suggested retaining the footprints of the former WTC towers, since this was such a deep concern of the groups representing the victims' families and friends. At the same time that these teams were working on their proposal, Stanton Eckstut of Ehrenkrantz Eckstut & Kuhn had been hired by the Port Authority as an urban design adviser to draw up a master plan for the site in cooperation with the LMDC, which some considered to be a mystifying overlap of efforts.

Regardless of the specifics given in the program, many observers pointed out how hypothetical it was, especially considering the lack of demand for office space and an uncertain retail market downtown. Richard Kahan, former head of the Battery Park City Authority, and president of Urban Assembly and Take the Field, bluntly said at *Architectural Record*'s panel discussion "Waiting for Ground Zero" on January 7, 2003, "There are two minor impediments—there's no program and no client." He was pointing not only to the ambiguity of the programmatic constraints, but to the ambiguous nature of client control: the land was owned by the Port Authority, the destroyed buildings had been leased to developer Larry Silverstein, and the replacement process was being administered by the LMDC and the Port Authority.

A realistic program and carefully thought-out phasing of the project was deemed to be crucial. The New York New Visions coalition evaluated the nine concepts from the seven teams in mid-January 2003. Hugh Hardy, chair of its Plan Review Task Force, said of the schemes, "If they are to be more than an illustration in an architectural history book, they must also be realistic—they must be able to be phased, to incorporate changing program needs and multiple participants over time, to fit within the context of the Lower Manhattan community." He forgot to say that the lines of power also would have to be changed.

TOP Greg Lynn of United Architects

CENTER Peter Eisenman, Charles Gwathmey, Richard Meier, and Steven Holl

LEFT Steven Peterson

ABOVE Barbara Littenberg

BELOW Site plan

BOTTOM Sketch showing how sunlight angles define shapes of two
parks

OPPOSITE View of the site model
from the south showing elevated
pathway and depressed memorial
space

INITIAL MASTER SITE PLAN

December 18, 2002

Studio Daniel Libeskind

**with Gary Hack, Hargreaves Associates,
and Jeff Zupan**

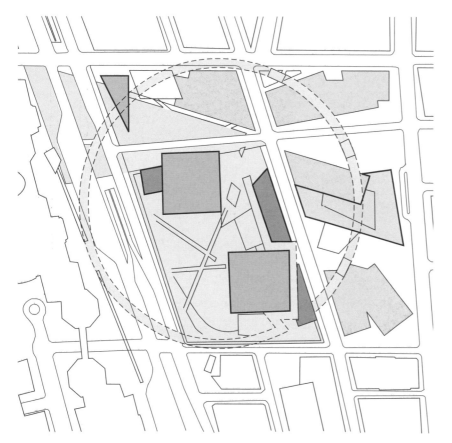

The master plan concept design "Memory Foundations," presented by Daniel Libeskind on December 18, 2002, grabbed the attention of the public with its tapering, asymmetrical spire extending 1,776 feet, and its humongous memorial space carved out of the site where the two towers stood. Revealed in this 70-foot-deep depression was the slurry wall of the original tower foundations, a grimly evocative trace that Libeskind saw as one of "the most dramatic elements to survive the attack." Hovering over the memorial space would be a prismatically shaped museum, and nearby were two public spaces called the "Park of Heroes" on the western side of the site, and the "Wedge of Light" on the east, plus an elevated curving walkway for memorial visitors that arced above and past West Street.

The Wedge of Light park was designed so that on September 11 sunlight could enter the memorial space between 8:46 A.M., when the first plane hit the north tower, and 10:28, when the north tower collapsed, the second to fall.

Other amenities and features of the plan included sky gardens at the top of the 1,776-foot-high tower above the sixty-fifth floor, with the spire beginning above the sixty-seventh floor. In addition there would be a performing arts center and a multilevel glazed structure between Greenwich and Church streets for the transit hub, with a below-grade rail station concourse to PATH trains and subways. The tops of a series of commercial towers on the eastern part of the site slanted toward the center, and the towers ascended in height from the south to the tall spire at the north. The plan kept Fulton Street (east-west), Greenwich Street (north-south), and added a landscaped promenade near Fulton Street that could take pedestrians to the Winter Garden and the World Financial Center. Gargantuan West Street remained a strong vehicular barrier between the two, however, and other east-west pedestrian links across the site seemed less apparent.

OPPOSITE As the view of the model from the west along the Hudson River shows, the plan calls for a series of commercial towers arrayed along the north and the east of the site

BELOW This section indicates relationship of various facilities to the open space; also of note is the detachment of the needle-like spire of the tallest tower from the office building component

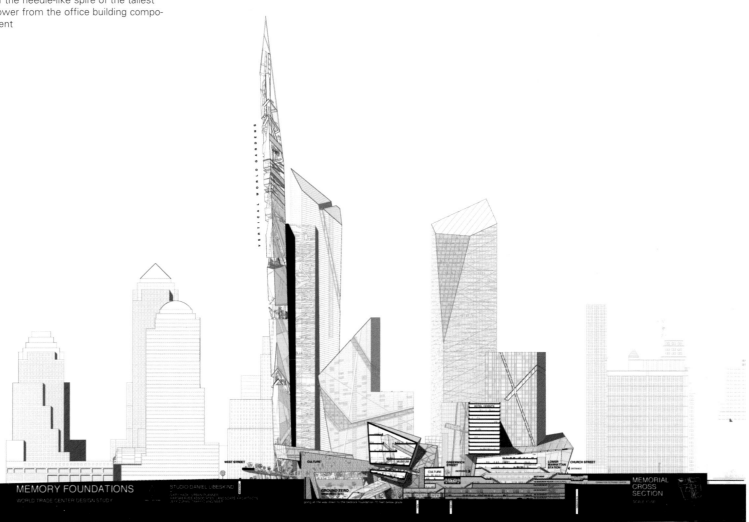

MEMORY FOUNDATIONS
WORLD TRADE CENTER DESIGN STUDY

STUDIO DANIEL LIBESKIND

MEMORIAL
CROSS
SECTION

While the scheme was criticized by the architectural community for a certain gimmickry with regard to the 1,776-foot height, or the severity of its gouged-out memorial space 70 feet below street level, these very aspects seemed to win support of the public. Similarly, the Wedge of Light was charged with being a public relations ploy, since the Millennium Hilton hotel going up nearby would effectively block eastern sunlight during those symbolic morning hours.

Nevertheless, the dynamism of the tower's asymmetrical spire, the curving walk, the transition of scale from low- to mid- to high-rise towers, combined with some rough surfaces and jagged forms, gave both a sense of vitality and a hard-edged, sober note to the complex. As some have noted, this dynamism was easiest to behold from a bird's-eye view. But the renderings displayed a forceful toughness that promised to keep the complex from looking like another office-tower-in-a-park scheme.

ABOVE The museum and the memorial space

RIGHT Section through the museum, showing access to the memorial space

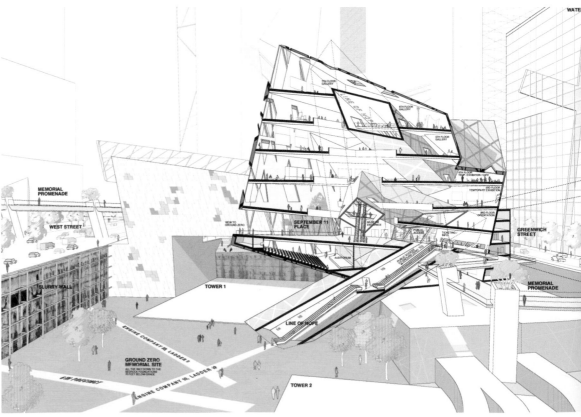

BELOW September 11th Place, focal point of site and location of anticipated cultural buildings; looking southwest through site

WINNING MASTER SITE PLAN

February 27, 2003

and

**MASTER SITE PLAN
WITH FINAL REFINEMENTS**

September 17, 2003

Studio Daniel Libeskind

When Studio Daniel Libeskind was selected
by the LMDC and the Port Authority on
February 27, 2003, the future seemed set.
Maybe not in stone, but certainly a strong
image emerged, even though it had already
been modified since the presentation
Libeskind made on December 18, 2002. But
now Libeskind's scheme had been selected
as the plan for the site by none other than
New York State Governor George Pataki.
There were, however, many questions
regarding Libeskind's precise role in the
process. Would his master plan determine
the actual development, architecture, and
urban design of the site? (The answer would
look more like "No" as time went on.) Would
other architects be called in to design various components? (Yes.)

In a battle that was only a taste of what was
to come, Libeskind had triumphed over the
THINK team, the other finalist from the
seven teams chosen by the LMDC for the
Innovative Design Study. Headed by Rafael
Viñoly, Frederic Schwartz, Shigeru Ban, and
landscape architect Ken Smith, THINK had
been favored by LMDC's site planning committee. But since Libeskind was the choice
of Governor Pataki, he was the ultimate
choice of the LMDC and Port Authority.

In vying for this honor, both teams had
reworked their earlier schemes. Libeskind's
updated plan demonstrated notable changes:
the curved elevated promenade that arced
around the west part of the site, connecting
to Battery Park City across West Street (page
54), had disappeared, for one. Libeskind
proposed that West Street could be
depressed with a park above it or kept at
grade and landscaped. Very noticeable was
his decision to raise the 70-foot-deep memorial park to an elevation only 30 feet below
street level, so that the slurry walls that had
created the "bathtub" for the foundations for
the WTC towers could be braced. (A memorial site at bedrock 70 feet down would still
remain.) The slurry wall was glassed over,
and, instead of bedrock, the open space was
planted with grass. The acute angles of the
towers seen December 2002 were now more

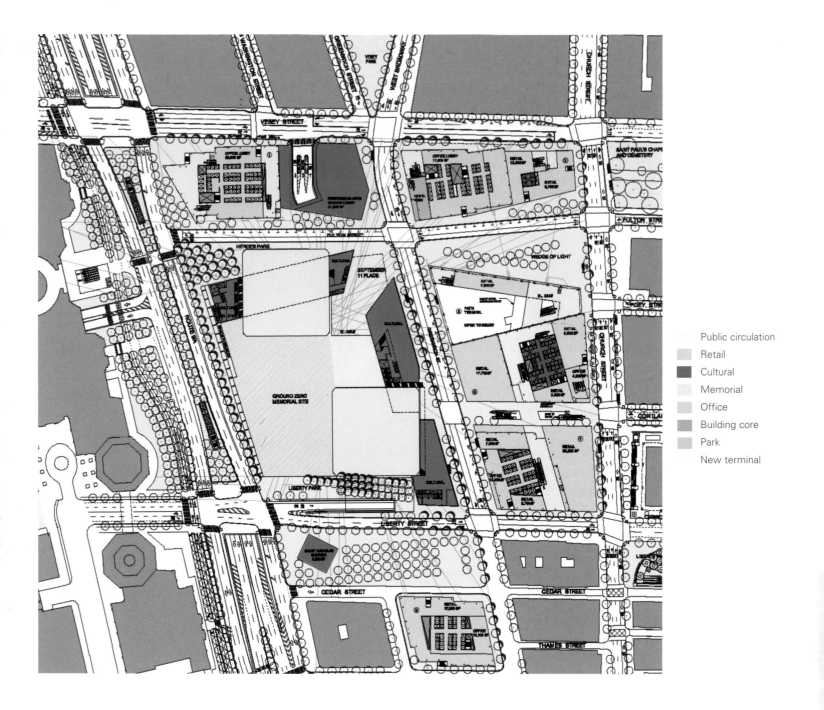

Public circulation

Retail

Cultural

Memorial

Office

Building core

Park

New terminal

ABOVE Site plan, September 17, 2003

OPPOSITE, TOP Wedge of Light plaza, Spring 2003

OPPOSITE, BOTTOM Park of Heroes, Spring 2003

regulated, not quite as skewed. The gardens in the sky in the spirelike 1,776-foot-high tower were gone, replaced by a restaurant and a transmission tower. Now more emphasis was given to the intersection of Fulton and Greenwich streets, the locus of the tower, a performing arts center, memorial museum, and the entrance to the transit station.

Over the ensuing months Libeskind quietly modified the plan some more before releasing on September 17, 2003, the "Refined Master Site Plan." By this date, the towers seen on February 27, 2003, had become taller, skinnier, and more shaftlike. Their footprints were less angled than earlier Libeskind schemes so that ground-level retail space paralleled the street line. A new two-square-block park was now included outside the boundaries of the WTC site, just south of Liberty Street, on property where the damaged Deutsche Bank building sits, and where the St. Nicholas Greek Orthodox

Church once stood. The additional park (if the owners of the property agreed to sell) would provide underground space for checking trucks delivering to the site, relieving the actual WTC site of that function.

Although key elements were intact, such as the 1,776-foot-high tower, the slurry wall, the Wedge of Light, and the Park of Heroes, it was clear they had been modified already or were jiggled a bit more.

At this time (September 13, 2003) the *New York Times* published comparative drawings of the plan as it evolved between September 2003 and the original presentation the previous December, clearly showing the "accommodations." For example, the Park of Heroes and the Wedge of Light had shriveled in size. Their placement around Fulton Street remained, but now Fulton was open possibly to buses instead of being given over entirely to pedestrians.

RIGHT Transportation hub, Spring 2003

BELOW Cultural facility, Spring 2003

As Edward Wyatt pointed out in the *Times*, the land-use pattern was quite similar to one of Beyer Blinder Belle's rejected "first-round" schemes, particularly "Memorial Plaza," incorporating a scheme that Cooper Robertson executed for Brookfield Properties (page 96).

Part of Libeskind's mandate was to come up with guidelines for the site, so that various architects commissioned to design the transportation hub, cultural facilities, or towers would have some parameters. On September 30, developer Larry Silverstein asked three international name-brand architects, Jean Nouvel, Fumihiko Maki, and Norman Foster, to design the towers along with SOM's David Childs, the lead architect for Freedom Tower. Since no precise dates were given for the towers' construction in a soft real estate market, this move was perceived by many observers as a public relations ploy.

Yet Libeskind's early drafts for the guidelines were deemed too specific to allow for individual (*other* individuals') architectural creativity. A draft dated October 23 and October 27, 2003, prescribed the towers' heights (beginning at 871 feet and moving

up to 1,776 feet), the distance of the towers from each other, and the angles at which each of the rooftops would slant. Tower configurations could be rectangular or trapezoidal: no curves or pyramids were allowed. Although stone or terra-cotta could be used in the lower part of the towers, metal and glass (white or gray) were mandated above.

The specificity of the guidelines resulted in protests from Herbert Muschamp of the *New York Times* that the glamorous architects brought in by Larry Silverstein would only be producing working drawings for their towers. His point is well taken—if indeed the stars being hired today by Silverstein are the ones who will be designing the towers when the market demand comes back. Nevertheless, since the Port Authority is not beholden to New York City zoning, the guidelines are a good idea in the long run, but the issue still awaits resolution.

TOP Lawn of memorial area, February 2003

ABOVE Refined master site plan, September 2003

THINK

Rafael Viñoly Architects, Frederic Schwartz Architects, Shigeru Ban Architect + Dean Maltz, Ken Smith Landscape Architect, William Morrish, Jane Marie Smith and Rockwell Group, plus engineers Büro Happold, Arup, and Jörg Schlaich of Schlaich Bergermann und Partner

The THINK team convinced the LMDC and the Port Authority to let them submit three schemes for this stage of the Innovative Design Study competition, making them the only team that submitted more than one scheme. This was not a great idea. The decision added much to the confusion at the December 18, 2002, presentation by Rafael Viñoly. The press and the public were not sure if the three were intended as separate proposals, or were meant to be placed simultaneously on the same site. (They were not.)

Of the three, one, the "World Cultural Center" (this page), stood out in both size and the degree of engineering required to make it work. Comprising two 1,665-foot-tall lattice structures of steel, built around the footprints of the former WTC towers, the scheme called for a memorial, a museum, a performing arts center, a conference center, and an amphitheater to be embedded within the open frame. Between the two towers would be located the transportation center, with retail space at the street and concourse levels. As an environmental consideration, two large-scale turbines would convert wind into electricity to power the center. The lattice towers rise from reflecting pools with glass bottoms to bring light into the concourse below grade. And at the approximate place where the planes hit, an abstracted twisted element literally ties the two buildings together. But as a symbolic connection to 9/11, it struck many as too gruesome a marker, and references to it were quickly downplayed after the December presentation.

Although the response to the World Cultural Center was positive, architectural observers had questions about the rest of the plan. Elevated walkways connected the two towers with the rest of the complex, and Greenwich and Fulton streets extended through the site, but the design of the nine commercial towers on the north, east, and south was left undefined. In the vast amount of effort, time, and money that went into developing three schemes for the site, this aspect of the

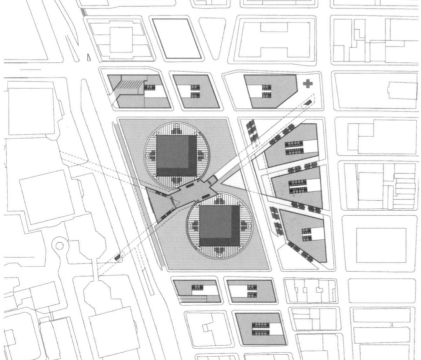

World Cultural Center

TOP Section showing cultural facilities embedded in lattice towers

ABOVE Site plan

OPPOSITE Steel lattice towers seen from the Hudson River

conceptual master plan was given less attention than it was given in the competitors' schemes. The obvious question was why present three schemes anyway, instead of combining resources and fully developing one persuasive scheme? The architects involved, Rafael Viñoly, Frederic Schwartz, and Shigeru Ban, and landscape architect Ken Smith, explained that each design represented different levels of public investment, from the most moderate, "Sky Park," to the "Great Room," and finally to the World Cultural Center. Nevertheless, in many minds the supposition remained that doing three schemes was the easiest way for a team with so many chefs and so little time to resolve any conflict. Shigeru Ban told *Architectural Record,* "Everyone presented

his own design or designs in the beginning. But the three schemes did not result from three architects' different views." Accordingly, Ban said he had worked the most on the Great Room scheme, while Viñoly developed the World Cultural Center from one of Ban's concept sketches. For his part, Ken Smith said he and Schwartz gave the most attention to the Sky Park.

World Cultural Center

OPPOSITE Views along Greenwich Street of THINK's World Cultural Center with elevated walkways connecting to the towers at the periphery of the site

BELOW An outdoor café is included near the World Cultural Center's observatory (approximately the fiftieth floor)

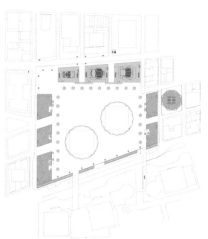

Great Room

The second scheme presented in December 2002, called the Great Room (aka Great Hall), displayed a 13-acre public space conceived as the world's largest covered public plaza (site plan, top left). The raised superblock is marked by two lattice-like circular silos with glass panels (left), which surround the footprints of the previous World Trade Center. The project has sustainable features, including stacking shutters that open to modulate the piazza's temperature. Office towers were arranged around the perimeter, with a tall tapering conical tower, extending 2,100 feet high on the southern end of the site (above). This transmission tower also houses offices and a hotel.

Sky Park

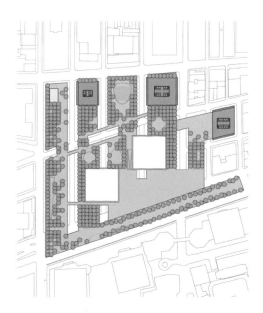

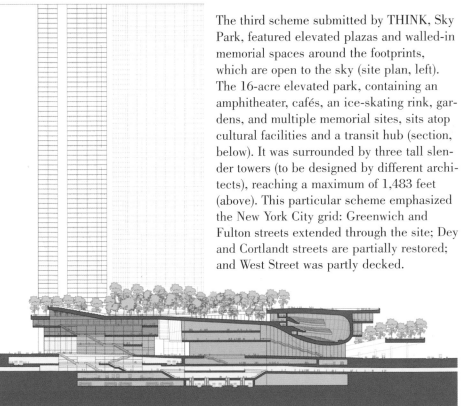

The third scheme submitted by THINK, Sky Park, featured elevated plazas and walled-in memorial spaces around the footprints, which are open to the sky (site plan, left). The 16-acre elevated park, containing an amphitheater, cafés, an ice-skating rink, gardens, and multiple memorial sites, sits atop cultural facilities and a transit hub (section, below). It was surrounded by three tall slender towers (to be designed by different architects), reaching a maximum of 1,483 feet (above). This particular scheme emphasized the New York City grid: Greenwich and Fulton streets extended through the site; Dey and Cortlandt streets are partially restored; and West Street was partly decked.

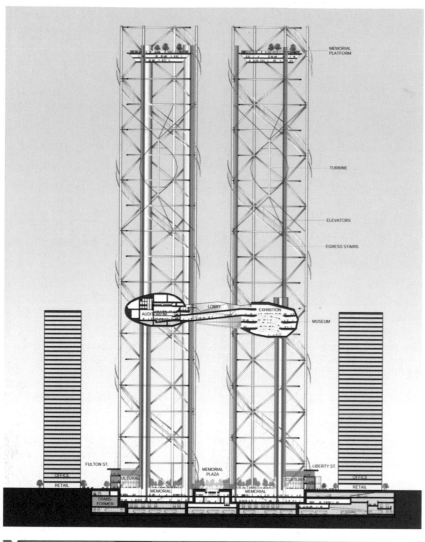

SECOND PLACE MASTER SITE PLAN

World Cultural Center

February 27, 2003

THINK

Rafael Viñoly Architects, Frederic Schwartz Architects, Shigeru Ban Architect + Dean Maltz, Ken Smith Landscape Architect, William Morrish, Jane Marie Smith and Rockwell Group, Büro Happold, with Jörg Schlaich of Schlaich Bergermann und Partner

The runner-up entry for the LMDC and the Port Authority's Innovative Design Study, THINK team's scheme for two lattice towers, presented December 18, 2002, appealed to a large segment of the public. Like Studio Daniel Libeskind's original scheme, THINK's World Cultural Center went through serious refinements and modifications before the decision to select Libeskind in February 2003. Working with engineer Jörg Schlaich of Schlaich Bergermann und Partner, the architects brought the lattice towers, which had been 1,665 feet high, down to 1,440 feet, and devised a way to construct them of a lighter-weight steel than the previous incarnation. If the towers were built of painted steel, they could cost an estimated $384 million; stainless steel would cost $415 million. A detailed account of construction techniques (such as stainless steel nodes, developed by Schlaich, that are welded to structural members with an automatic machine) and the method of erection was submitted with the scheme.

The refined lattice towers were thinner and less encumbered than the December prototype, with fewer cultural elements suspended in their shafts. The museum was shifted from the seventieth floor to the thirty-fifth floor, and a park instead of a reflecting pool surrounded the towers at grade. A glazed transportation terminal faces Church Street.

TOP World Cultural Center, section

ABOVE World Cultural Center, site plan

RIGHT Glazed transportation hub

OPPOSITE World Cultural Center from the Hudson River

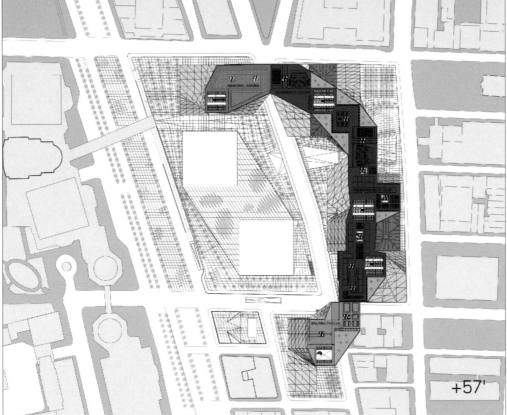

December 18, 2002

United Architects

Foreign Office Architects (Farshid Moussavi and Alejandro Zaera-Polo), Greg Lynn FORM, Kevin Kennon Architects, Reiser + Umemoto RUR Architecture, Imaginary Forces NYC (Mikon van Gastel, Peter Frankfurt), and UN Studio (Ben van Berkel, Caroline Bos) with engineers Thornton-Tomasetti, and Arup

The most unusual scheme presented on December 18, 2002, was the Brobdingnagian megastructure dreamed up by United Architects, an ad hoc consortium of avant-garde firms from Amsterdam, London, Los Angeles, and New York.

What appears to be a single building snaking around the northern, eastern, and southern edges of the WTC site is five structurally independent but connected towers. As it looms higher, it seems to hover over the memorial area—the footprints of the two World Trade Center towers—in a protective stance. The tallest of the towers is 1,620 feet; altogether, these structures would provide more than 10 million square feet of floor area. The buildings are linked by a skyway, 800 feet above the ground, and sky gardens are sprinkled throughout the com-

TOP View from the Hudson River with Battery Park City and the World Financial Center in the foreground

ABOVE Site plan at 57 feet above grade

OPPOSITE Model showing building linked by skyway

plex on every five floors. The plan also calls
for a sky memorial at the peak of the towers,
along with a memorial at the footprints. The
buildings come with many exit doors, in case
of fire or other disasters, and the architects
even include areas of refuge every thirty
floors. The transit hub, placed underground,
surfaces at Church Street, while Greenwich
Street extends through the site.

The sheer bravado and muscular energy of
the scheme impressed many of the viewers
seeing it for the first time on December 18,
and its dramatic posture makes one wonder,
What if the thing starts to walk? Generally,
however, its density (King Kong meets Hong
Kong) was hard to fully warm up to, even for
New Yorkers—for now. It may indeed be a
harbinger of the future.

OPPOSITE In the memorial space, visitors descend a spiral walkway 75 feet below grade, then look up from the footprints of the former WTC towers to the behemoths rising dramatically above

RIGHT From the towers visitors can gaze down upon the footprints with a vertiginous perspective

BELOW Viewed from Park Row near City Hall Park, the complex bursts out from its staid, physical context, which includes the Woolworth Tower (far right in photograph), designed by Cass Gilbert in 1913

Foster and Partners

with engineers Cantor Seinuk Group

Norman Foster's proposal for twin towers envisions 1,764-foot-tall geometrical monoliths conjoined in three places and outfitted with observation platforms and sky parks. The two towers, with a multilayered facade to permit natural ventilation for most of the year, occupy the eastern edge of the site, overlooking the footprints of the World Trade Center towers to the west. The footprints themselves become empty voids, bounded by walls of steel and stone, while elsewhere landscaped open spaces dominate, including a park bridging West Street to Battery Park City and the Hudson River. Fulton and Greenwich streets extend through the site, and Liberty Street becomes a street market.

The scheme received strong public support, especially from those who saw it as an up-to-date variant on the former WTC towers. Urban design and architecture critics noted that the ground plane was undeveloped with the exception of the trees.

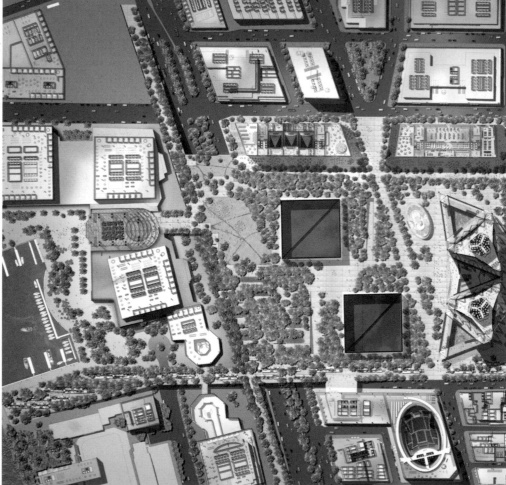

TOP View from the East River

ABOVE Site plan

OPPOSITE View from the Hudson River

LEFT Transportation center with a glass canopy and a below-grade concourse connecting PATH trains, subway lines, and airtrain links to major airports

BELOW Memorial spaces in footprints bound by glass-and-steel walls and open to the sky

BOTTOM Park around memorial walls of footprints

OPPOSITE Section and rendering showing relationship of towers to below-grade facilities

December 18, 2002

**Richard Meier & Partners,
Eisenman Architects,
Gwathmey Siegel &
Associates, and Steven
Holl Architects with
engineers Craig Schwitter/
Büro Happold**

BELOW View from the East River

OPPOSITE View from the Hudson River

In the most abstracted scheme presented, the team of Richard Meier, Peter Eisenman, Charles Gwathmey, and Steven Holl, along with their respective partners and offices, worked together on a gridded megastructure. Two structures with five towers contain a mix of uses—9 million square feet for offices, a hotel, a convention center, and cultural facilities—in buildings that rise 1,111 feet and occupy only 25 percent of the site. The configuration of the towers makes sky gardens possible, along with interconnected superfloors for trading or conventions. Photovoltaic cells in the walls enable sunlight to be trapped and to emit a glow at night, as these views from the East River and Hudson River indicate. The buildings edge the WTC footprints on the north and east, their gridlike pattern repeating the grid of the streets. Shallow glass-bottomed reflecting pools occupy the footprints of the original towers.

The team designed the project to feature a large Memorial Plaza, and they decked over West Street so that fingers of open space extend west to the Hudson River. As part of this notion, the shadows that would have been cast by the original WTC towers are demarcated by groves of trees and paving.

The team's scheme seemed too unremittingly pure to go over with the general public. It also incited much discussion about the joint "signature" of the four design architects. While Peter Eisenman argued that ultimately the project didn't look like any of the firms' individual styles, the traces are there from each of the team member's past work.

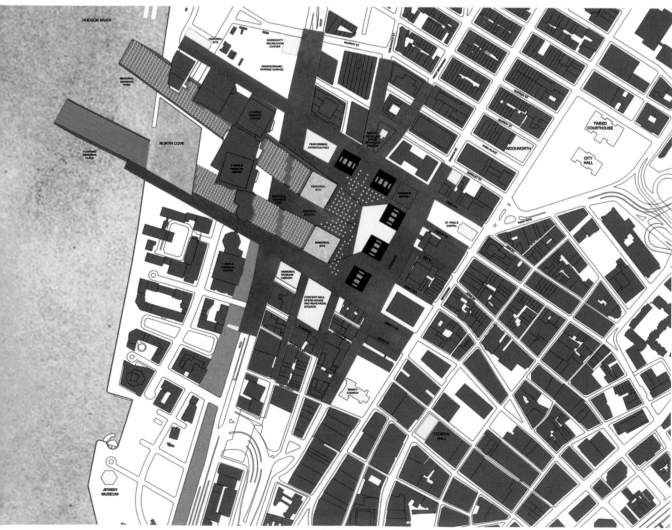

OPPOSITE, TOP View from the Hudson River

OPPOSITE, BOTTOM Site plan

RIGHT Orthogonal drawing shows the extension of fingers of open space to the Hudson River: the landscaped swaths indicate the shadow lines of the original WTC towers, while red paving extends other parts of the grid emanating from the plaza

BOTTOM View from the north

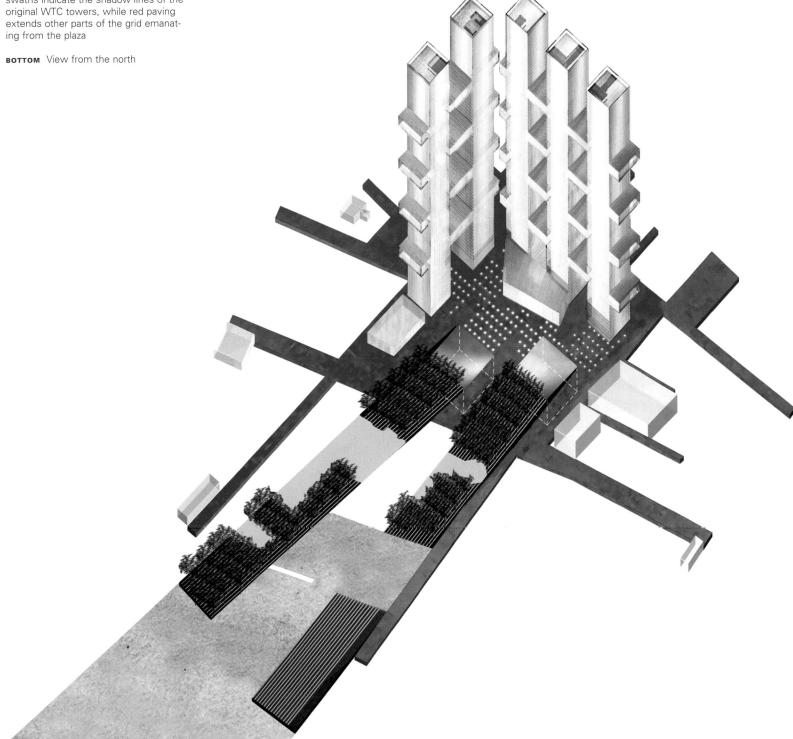

December 18, 2002

Skidmore, Owings & Merrill (SOM)

with SANAA (Kazuyo Sejima and Ryue Nishizawa), Iñigo Manglano-Ovalle, Rita McBride, Field Operations (Stan Allen and James Corner), Michael Maltzan Architecture, Tom Leader Studio, Neutelings Riedijk (initial participants), Jessica Stockholder, and Elyn Zimmerman

In many ways the scheme the SOM team proposed was the most radical. Instead of towers arranged discreetly to the north and east around the WTC footprints, a dense grid of nine 940-foot-high towers, with 13 million square feet of commercial office space, march across the site, on parcels of land bounded by the major surrounding thoroughfares (Fulton, Greenwich, Vesey, and West streets). Reflecting pools with bridges cover the footprints of the original towers. Gardens, totaling 16 acres, are located at the top of each tower, and green spaces naturally exchange carbon dioxide for oxygen, one of several environmental features.

The proposal was viewed by the architectural community as brave, but strange in its deployment of density with a cluster of bent vertical structures, where none rises majestically above the skyline. Also, the location of so many gardens in the sky made some wonder if mothers with strollers would want to take the time to go through building security to travel upstairs to visit them. The amount and size of the reflecting pools seemed to other observers to give too much of a role to water: not a pleasant amenity on cold, windy, or icy days. The analysis by the New York New Visions group ("Evaluation of Innovative Design Proposals January 2003") brought up some more intriguing problems. The report pointed out that the "herd of towers" would present two marketing problems: one caused by the obstruction of views, reducing leasing value; and a lack of differentiation in the type of tower, offering little flexibility for varying tenant needs.

The team was led by SOM designer Roger Duffy, who had invited the various members to take part. The idea of bringing together a number of artists to work with architects was ambitious. Besides SOM and SANAA, architects included Stan Allen, from Field Operations, and Michael Maltzan, in addition to Rotterdam architects Willem Neutelings and Michael Riedijk, who eventually withdrew over disagreement with the plan. But the collaborative effort seemed to result in a scheme that needed more resolu-

STREET LEVEL

tion in the ground level areas, or at least more development in the presentation of those ideas.

The inclusion of SOM by the LMDC in the Innovative Design Study also spurred suspicion: SOM's David Childs had been working on a plan the previous summer with Larry Silverstein, the developer with the lease for the site. Also, Childs is the architect for the 7 World Trade Center tower, which is already being built just north of the site. In order to participate in this competition, SOM had to suspend work for Silverstein during this particular phase. And even David Childs and Marilyn Taylor, the two heads of the SOM New York office, felt they should not take part in this innovative design competition.

So it seemed even more perplexing when, right after the December 2002 presentation, SOM decided to withdraw from the team in order to continue working for its first client, Silverstein. SOM argued that it expected the LMDC would allow the rest of the team to continue to the next phase of cost and traffic analyses. But the LMDC said if SOM was out, the whole team was out. And that was that. Another theory? Although SOM knew it would have to pull out, it wanted to float an alternate (and artier) plan to see what the reaction would be. In any event, this scheme did not meet with tremendous success.

ABOVE View from East River

OPPOSITE, TOP The gardens on the tops of the towers

OPPOSITE, BOTTOM Site plan

OPPOSITE Sky bridges connecting the nine towers, and linking various indoor gardens

BELOW A skylit transit hub located between Church and Greenwich, and Fulton and Liberty streets, with primary access through Church Street

December 18, 2002

Peterson/Littenberg Architecture and Urban Design

The New York–based firm of Peterson/ Littenberg Architecture and Urban Design, in-house consultants on contract for the LMDC, were asked by the agency to submit a master plan for the WTC site, along with the six teams selected by competition. Many tiny-eyed observers viewed this seventh team as a group of outsiders—or, more problematic, ultra-insiders. Neither status proved to be helpful to the firm in the end.

The scheme proposed by Steven Peterson and Barbara Littenberg calls for two 1,400-foot-tall mixed-use towers and five other towers to be placed around sunken memorial gardens, a quiet pedestrian precinct, in which the footprint of the south tower is demarcated by a reflecting pool. The original footprint of the north WTC tower becomes the locus of an amphitheater where each seat

commemorates a victim of 9/11. A museum is placed underneath the amphitheater, and the main transit hub is situated between the two eastern towers. The distinction of the plan is its emphasis on streets, with activities on both sides, and its restored street grid. Unlike other schemes, here Greenwich Street is straightened to allow a two-sided street without impinging on the footprint of the former south WTC tower. In the grandest gesture of the urban design plan, the architects decked over the express lanes of West Street between Vesey and Liberty streets, treating it as a landscaped boulevard from Liberty Street to Battery Place.

This feature had appeared in an earlier scheme Peterson/Littenberg presented in the first round of LMDC/Port Authority proposals in July 2002 (page 101), along with

Beyer Blinder Belle's entries, where it received much praise from the general public. In this scheme, Peterson/Littenberg includes four theaters, a library, a school, 500,000 square feet of housing (in the mixed-use towers), and 1 million square feet of retail area within the 16-acre site.

The long axial boulevard, the monument at the intersection of Liberty and West streets, and the tapering towers of the skyscrapers bring to mind the early-twentieth-century City Beautiful movement and the skyscraper forms that developed from the early twentieth century to the 1930s. This backward glance to the oldies but goodies in urban design and architecture, however, did not sit well with a lot of architecture critics who felt this was a moment for experimentation and innovation.

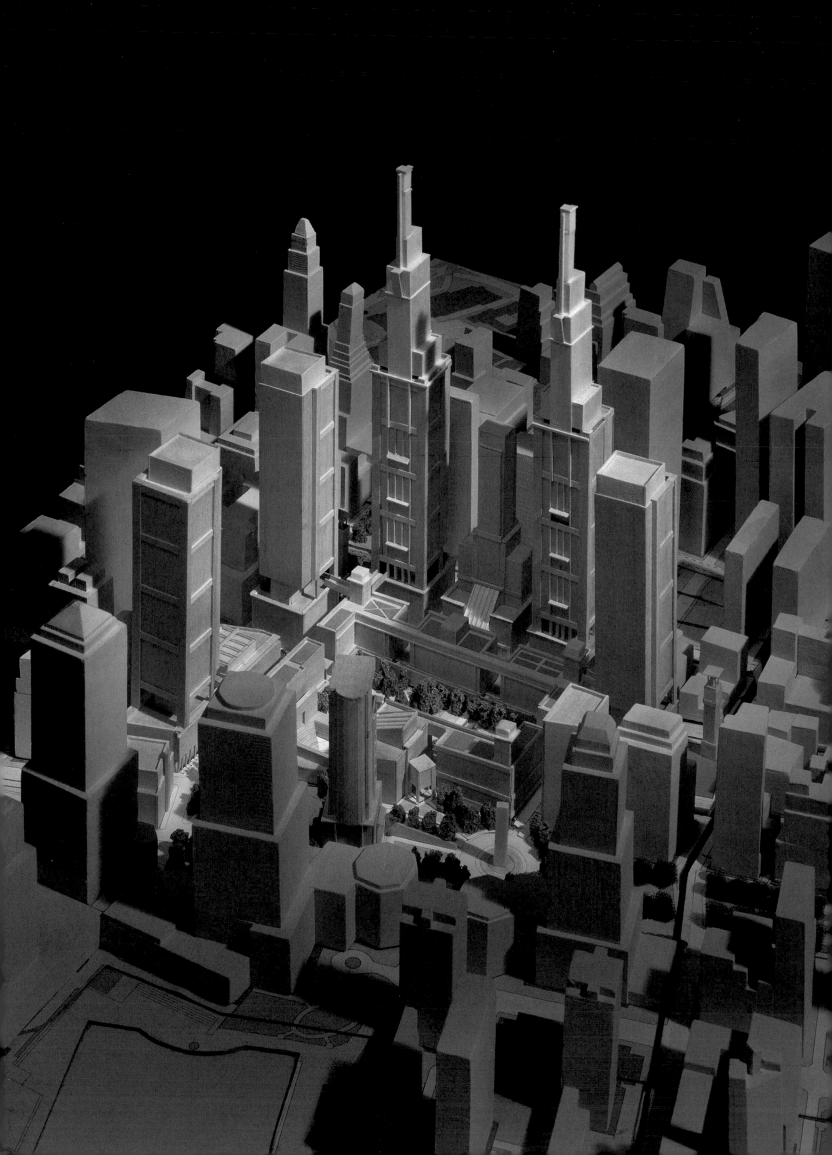

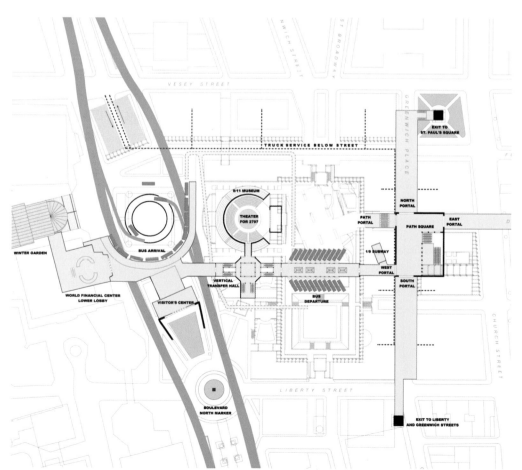

Peterson/Littenberg countered that their scheme was not meant to be about architectural style, but the urban design principles that served as part of New York's tradition. Nevertheless, their efforts were seen as palliative: the LMDC had included Peterson/Littenberg as a way of placating those who might argue for a more contextual response to New York City's landscape. If the architects felt clobbered by being branded as retardataire by the architecture community, they were able to console themselves that Libeskind's more radical vision got chipped away over time.

Open Space,
Open Space,
Primarily Ho
existing
Primarily Ho
proposed
Primarily Cor
existing
Primarily Cor
proposed
Civic and Ins
existing
Civic and Ins
proposed

OPPOSITE Two twin stepped-back towers and other shorter ones arranged around the sunken gardens

ABOVE Site plan showing memorial boulevard that extends to the southern tip of Manhattan and a transit hub between the two tall towers

LEFT Below-grade plan with a bus arrival zone just west of the amphitheater in an area that had once been West Street—visitors can walk south under cover and, because of the topographical changes in grade, emerge at ground level at the rotary at Liberty Place, and then continue walking down the promenade to Battery Park

BELOW John H. Beyer of Beyer Blinder Belle

BOTTOM Concept sketch by John H. Beyer for planning study commissioned by the Battery Park City Authority about improving linkages between Battery Park City and downtown

First Round in the Planning Process

July 2002

BELOW John H. Beyer of Beyer Blinder Belle

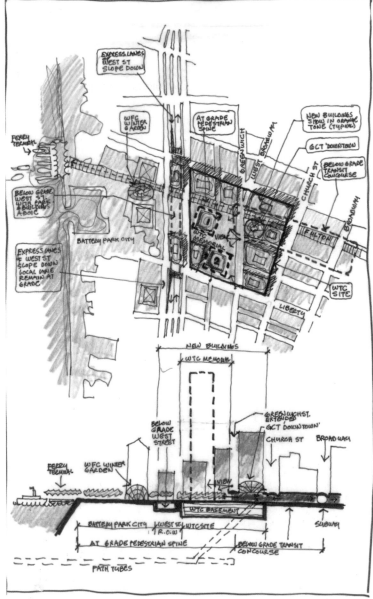

BOTTOM Concept sketch by John H. Beyer for planning study commissioned by the Battery Park City Authority about improving linkages between Battery Park City and downtown

In the process of rebuilding downtown, the confusion over the exact definition of the term *master plan* was first brought into high relief in the summer of 2002. In May, Beyer Blinder Belle (BBB) and engineers Parsons Brinkerhoff were named by the LMDC and the Port Authority as the master planners for the World Trade Center site.

The firm was essentially asked to come up with a land-use and transportation plan for the 16-acre site, including 11 million square feet of office space, 450,000 to 600,000 square feet of retail space, and a 600,000-square-foot hotel in addition to memorial space. BBB began working on a half-dozen variations, placing basic building blocks mostly to the northern and eastern edges of the site to show alternatives for the various office towers. Usually they left the footprints of the towers for a park or some sort of noncommercial space.

But BBB soon found out that being selected for this highly publicized role had its drawbacks. The public (and even members of the architectural community) generally assumed that blocks representing buildings in their models were being mandated—as architecture—not as illustrations of land-use and bulk guidelines. Although BBB had garnered much acclaim for its restorations of Ellis Island (1991) and Grand Central Terminal (1998), the firm is not as reputed for its new architecture as for its renovation work, nor is its urban design reputation as high-profile as other firms.

Nevertheless, BBB was the lead urban designer for a little-known task-force study of West Street—the street that splits the WTC site from Battery Park City—commissioned by the Battery Park City Authority during the winter of 2002. Beyer's sketches for the area included the WTC site, and the land-use diagram, conceived months before the Lower Manhattan Development Corporation chose BBB to do the master plan, explains why the firm seemed like such a natural choice. Another significant factor in the selection was that BBB's engineers, Parsons Brinkerhoff, had been involved with transportation infrastructure in Battery Park City. But attacks on BBB in the press about its lack of innovation in terms of design helped reinforce the public belief that the issues at hand were primarily architectural, not planning ones.

It is true that innovative architecture (especially in New York) gets short shrift. Indeed, in this first round, most of the architects on the six teams who competed against BBB were part of the establishment. (To be considered, the architects responding to the Request for Qualifications sent out by the LMDC and the

Port Authority had to have worked on at least three $100 million projects. Fifteen teams initially submitted, and of these, six, including BBB, were selected for further interviews.) The teams had solid urban design experience, but their varied architectural reputations promised more home cooking, rather than the haute cuisine of the international set. Besides BBB, one team was composed of Kohn Pedersen Fox (with engineers Arup and architect Frederic Schwartz, among others); another had Hardy Holzman Pfeiffer, Fox and Fowle, Gruzen Samton (with engineers STV Group and DMJM + Harris); another, Ehrenkrantz, Eckstut & Kuhn (with engineers URS); a fifth, Robert A. M. Stern Architects (with Earth Tech/TAMS engineers); and finally Rem Koolhaas and Davis Brody Bond (with Arup as engineers).

Rem Koolhaas was arguably the only avant-garde (and international star) architect on the list. Behind-the-scenes rumors had it that Koolhaas and his team didn't win because he was not considered the personable type that could build a consensus among the public. In the choice of BBB the LMDC and the Port Authority may well have been counting on the affable styles of two of its principals, John H. Beyer and John Belle, to carry the day. "This is a process requiring patience," explained one architect who interviewed for the job. "You're going to deal with community groups and agencies. You need an architect who knows how to put up with all this stuff."

It must have been a surprise that Beyer Blinder Belle's schemes got clobbered when presented to over 4,300 New Yorkers in the Town Hall meeting at the Javits Center on July 20, 2002, organized by the Civic Alliance to Rebuild Downtown New York. But something already was going wrong with the process that could inspire sympathy for BBB, no matter what one thought of the schemes. The architects (and the press) were given the impression that, once chosen, BBB had about six weeks to come up with six schemes. Then three of those schemes would be narrowed down for a September presentation, with one being selected by the end of the year. Just before the July presentation, BBB was informed that Peterson/Littenberg would be showing two of their schemes as part of the six. Furthermore, the two independent plans for the site executed not for the LMDC, but for private developers, one by Cooper Robertson for Brookfield Financial Properties, the other by David Childs of SOM for Larry Silverstein, would also be incorporated into BBB's presentation.

Quitting was not an option for BBB in terms of getting future work from the Port Authority. So BBB stayed—and Beyer prop-

erly and ethically made it clear at the July 16 presentation that two of the schemes were Peterson/Littenberg's, and two reflected the input from Cooper Robertson and SOM.

However, Beyer did not explain forcefully enough at the presentation that the visual information was basically bulk and land-use diagrams. The public thought all the schemes, with the exception of Peterson/Littenberg's "Memorial Promenade," with its long axial boulevard to Battery Place, were banal. The public and the press looked at the boxy unarticulated shapes, and assumed that what you see is what you get (which in New York can be a strong possibility).

The high square footage requirement of 11 million proved to be a lightning rod as well. As soon as the firestorm started over the lack of architecture, the LMDC began to back down on the square footage required. It helped that the economic prophecies for downtown real estate were grim: it probably would be years before that amount of office space could be leased.

In August, BBB stated that it had actually developed a dozen different alternatives in the first six weeks, "many of which went beyond the initial program restraints. We regret that our most creative work from this period was not presented for public view." By then it was too late. The firm was effectively eliminated.

Many observers would blame the LMDC program for overloading office space in the program: in the next round LMDC would trim it to a range of 6.5 million to 10 million square feet to try to satisfy its lease obligations to Larry Silverstein. But more significant than the quantity of office space allowed was the basic disposition of commercial space around the north, east, and part of the south of the former footprints for the WTC towers (increasingly understood as sacrosanct memorial space), with the transit hub on the east. This plan was basic to BBB's schemes (and to Cooper Robertson's plan for Brookfield Financial Properties), and would remain an influential template for the future.

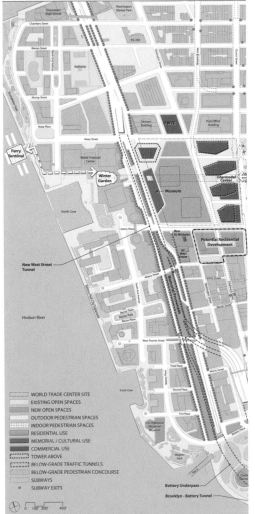

MEMORIAL PLAZA Concept Plan 1

Beyer Blinder Belle

This plan, which incorporated the contribution of Cooper Robertson & Partners for Brookfield Financial Properties, also shows the legacy of Beyer's own concept sketch for Battery Park City in February 2002. It places four trapezoid-shaped towers from sixty-two to seventy-nine stories in height around the eastern edge, where a transportation center is located (top). The footprints of the two original WTC towers are intact, along with an 8-acre plaza and a memorial cultural building on the west side. The express lanes of West Street are below grade; at grade is open space for the public, so that a total of 18.1 acres of new public space are created (site plan, left). Greenwich Street continues through the site, although Fulton and Cortlandt streets only partially extend through it. This and the following plans include a 1,500-foot-tall "skyline element" (above).

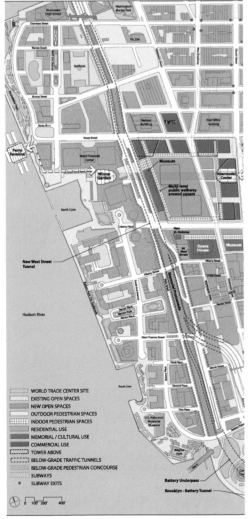

MEMORIAL SQUARE Concept Plan 2

Beyer Blinder Belle

Beyer Blinder Belle's scheme calls for a 10-acre square with a memorial/cultural building along the west side of the site, keeping the footprints of the towers free, and placing four towers on the east and north sides of the site (site plan, left). One tower would be eighty stories high, two would be seventy stories, and one would be fifty-six stories (top). Along the south portion of the site (across Liberty Street) are cultural facilities, while Liberty Street is a green corridor extending from Broadway west to the waterfront, West Street is buried in a tunnel, and Greenwich Street is extended through the site. The plan calls for a total of 24.1 acres of public space, including a promenade.

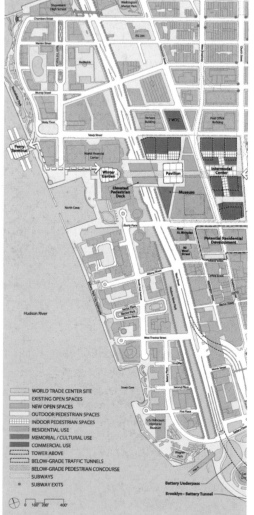

MEMORIAL TRIANGLE Concept Plan 3

Beyer Blinder Belle

Beyer Blinder Belle has generated a triangular space, five acres in size (site plan, left). A public pavilion sits in the footprint of the north tower, and an elevated deck bridges over West Street to connect the site to the Winter Garden of the World Financial Center. West Street remains at grade, Greenwich Street extends through the site, and there are six towers in all: one is eighty-five stories, one is sixty-one stories, and four are fifty-nine stories high (top). The area south of Liberty Street is designated for potential residential development. Indoor pedestrian spaces link much of the site.

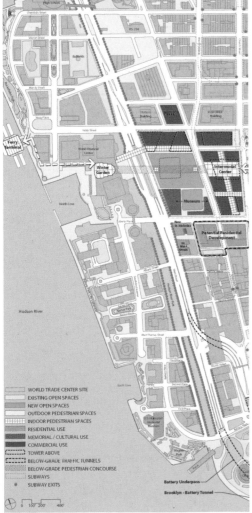

MEMORIAL GARDEN Concept Plan 4

Beyer Blinder Belle

This version, influenced by the design that Skidmore, Owings & Merrill executed for its private client, the site's leaseholder, Larry Silverstein, calls for five towers, again placed on the northern and eastern edge of the site (top, and site plan, left). The tallest is eighty stories, two are sixty-six stories, and two are fifty stories high. A museum occupies the south footprint, and an underground concourse extends through the north footprint linking the intermodal transportation center with the Winter Garden of the World Financial Center on the other side of West Street.

Peterson/Littenberg
Architecture and Urban Design

Peterson/Littenberg Architecture and Urban Design developed this scheme as consultants for the LMDC. Many of the streets in the city's grid are brought back (site plan, bottom left), and memorial and cultural uses, along with open space, occupy the site of the World Trade Center. The footprints are not emphasized (left), but the area remains open. Five commercial towers, three at forty-five stories, and two at seventy-five stories, are clustered around the park. West Street is partially decked over, and Fulton and Cortlandt streets both continue to the World Financial Center. Like the Beyer Blinder Belle plans, this plan includes a 1,500-foot-tall "skyline element."

Peterson/Littenberg
Architecture and Urban Design

Peterson/Littenberg designed a grand promenade to be the main feature of this alternate scheme: extending from Liberty Street to Battery Park along West Street, it is created by placing West Street in a tunnel from Vesey Street to Battery Park (right). From the promenade, visitors gain access to the cultural and memorial functions that occupy the western part of the site. The footprints of the WTC towers remain (site plan, bottom right), but as open park space.

Most of the commercial development occurs on the north and east: six towers are planned—two are sixty-three stories, four are thirty-two, and there are two 1,500-foot-high skyline elements. The overall plan accentuates the large public space as a destination embedded in the street grid. Accordingly, Greenwich Street and West Broadway are merged on the north, with Greenwich then bending through the site where it becomes Washington Street on the south. Church Street on the east is the major downtown artery, while Fulton and Liberty streets extend as east-west connectors through the site.

Cooper Robertson & Partners

for Brookfield Financial Properties

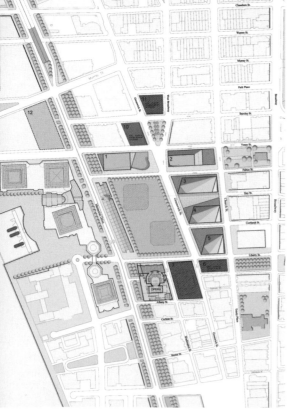

Just as the LMDC and the Port Authority were in the process of selecting Beyer Blinder Belle to come up with the master plan for the World Trade Center site, Brookfield Financial Properties, which owns the World Financial Center next door, decided to take some initiative. John Zuccotti, the chairman of Brookfield Properties, and, incidentally, the former chair of the New York City Planning Commission and a former deputy mayor, asked Cooper Robertson to draw up a plan for the 16-acre WTC site. Although Brookfield is a private developer with no legitimate governance over the site, it does control 8 million square feet of property downtown, which may or may not benefit from the WTC development facing it on the other side of West Street. The plan restores Greenwich and Fulton streets, which ran through the site before the World Trade Center towers, and buries West Street in a tunnel. Like the other schemes, it concentrates the commercial office development around the northern and eastern portions of the site, leaving the footprints of the former towers clear for a memorial site of about 7 acres. It also includes cultural uses south of the memorial, and calls for the landmark building by Cass Gilbert at 90 West Street to be demolished. In addition, the plan calls for a rail link for LIRR commuters and a direct rail connection to Kennedy Airport.

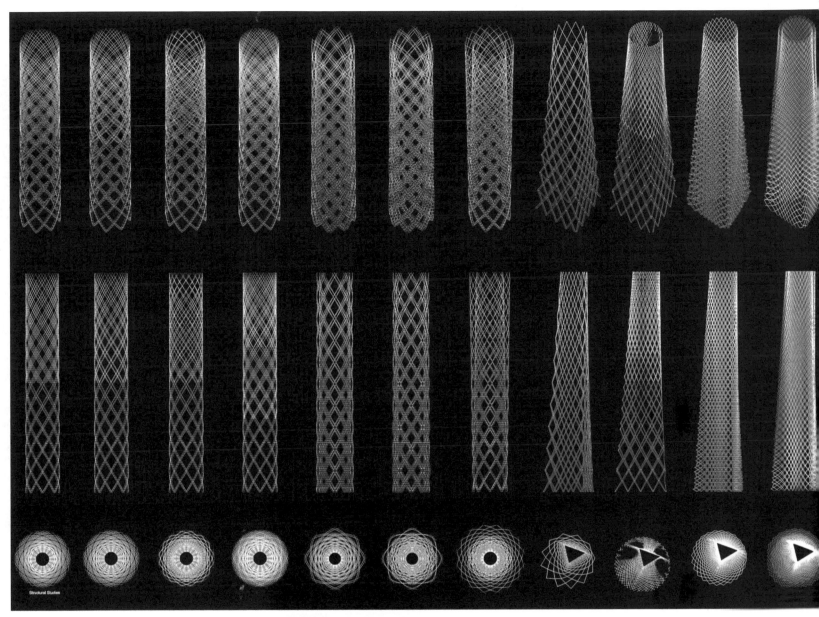

Structural Studies

David Childs/SOM

for Silverstein Properties

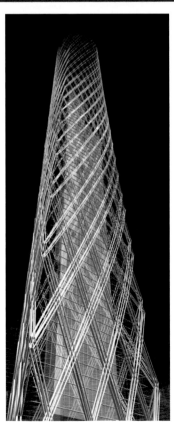

Larry Silverstein, who took over the lease to the World Trade Center in summer 2001, decided to have David Childs—with whom he was already working—develop a plan for the WTC site. At one point Silverstein and Brookfield Properties joined forces, but when it became clear that their architects had different approaches, each decided to produce a separate plan to encourage the LMDC to move ahead with redevelopment.

The tallest tower in Childs's plan has a triangular base. Slated for a site on Greenwich Street over the transit hub, it tapers as it rises into a circle at the top of a lattice steel structure. It is not hard to detect an affinity to Freedom Tower—that is, the spireless Freedom Tower that Childs wanted.

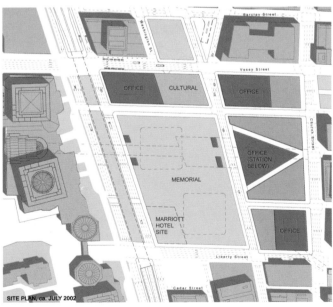

SITE PLAN, ca. JULY 2002

Press-Generated Proposals

The *New York Times Magazine* and *New York* Magazine

The press was generally critical of the official choices for the various stages of the rebuilding process from the moment that the first-round architects, Beyer Blinder Belle, had been announced in late spring 2002. The fear prevailed that talented, risk-taking architects would not be included in the rebuilding, that state and city officials would favor the same architects they had always worked with. The result would be bland, conventional, and cater too much to established real estate and government interests.

The architecture critics from two publications, Herbert Muschamp of the *New York Times*, and Joseph Giovannini of *New York* magazine, decided to not just kvetch and whine from the sidelines, but to actually do something. They each summoned some of the best talents of the day (with some overlap) to come up with schemes for their respective publications.

The press-sponsored teams had a singular advantage over the official designs being carried out by the Lower Manhattan Development Corporation and the Port Authority of New York and New Jersey: They could formulate their own programs. They did not have to abide by given square footage for commer-

cial, cultural, memorial, and transit uses; and they could actively seek to generate residential development, something explicitly not part of the Port Authority's purview.

The results were indeed provocative and imaginative. Freedom within the parameters established by the particular magazine proved to be a proper stimulant to the imagination.

By all accounts, Muschamp's team, which had started as a small group of dissatisfied architects and engineers meeting in June, was first; Giovannini's collection of individual participants followed soon after. They emerged at the same time, marking the first anniversary of the events of September 11, 2001. Of the two, the *New York Times* team was the larger. Because of its extensively developed program, the overall scheme most closely approached the form of a city plan that could be realized, given the proper budget and cooperative clients, both public and private. It showed the variegated responses accruing from a team collaboration on a large-scale master plan. Working with a large piece of lower Manhattan from the World Trade Center site down West Street, the team devised a land-use plan and an urban design scheme for

the area, and then assigned different architects various building types for the site.

By contrast Giovannini's *New York* magazine group acted on an individual basis, each coming up with their own distinct large-scale plans and schemes—or fantasies—for the site. Freedom from constraints nevertheless brought forth ideas that could prefigure designs of future cities and buildings.

It should be mentioned that the involvement of critics in coming up with schemes was controversial. The thought that architecture critics would round up architects to generate visions for the site instead of just sticking to printed criticism of official schemes rankled some observers. They felt that the critic was crossing an important line in becoming an advocate of designs he or she had helped bring into being. Architecture has a long history of the critic (Reyner Banham, Lewis Mumford) acting as the outspoken advocate of a particular direction. Still, there are many architects who believe "You can't run with the hare and hunt with the hound." In all it should be said that the extent of the creative output displayed in both press offerings was impressive and varied.

Rafael Viñoly
New York City

Transit Hub
Church Street between Fulton Street
and Cortlandt Street

Rafael Viñoly's Transit Hub at Church and Fulton streets seamlessly interweaves ten levels of concourses and ramps. The design for the transit hub offers a new vision for this type of facility by blurring the zone between the largely subterranean world of urban transport and the street above. Two subway lines, the PATH train to New Jersey, and taxi and bus service at street level fuse in a single interchange that facilitates ease of pedestrian movement and connection among the transit systems. Glass enclosures provide shelter from the elements to pedestrians while maintaining a transparent visual connection between the station's component parts and the immediate neighborhood.

Section looking west

Rem Koolhaas/OMA
Rotterdam, Netherlands, and New York City

Mixed-Use Towers
West Street between Liberty Street
and Albany Street

Rem Koolhaas and Joshua Ramus's contribution to the West Street design study suggests a fundamental rethinking of the skyscraper type. The wedding-cake section of the Downtown Athletic Club, built in 1931—and so memorably discussed in Koolhaas's *Delirious New York* (1978)—is flipped on its head, extruded, and multiplied to create a tripartite, sixty-story, mixed-use building.

Rather than setting back from the street as the building rises, this skyscraper meets the ground in the form of three slender columns, providing pedestrian access through West Street. The building's segments expand through a series of inverted setbacks, eventually merging to provide a maximum of space, natural light, and views on the upper floors. Supplementing a generous office program, hotel rooms and apartments keep the buildings functioning twenty-four hours a day. A roof garden reinforces the notion of inversion by creating a place for trees to take root 600 feet above the ground.

The structure of the building requires the application of a novel form of elevator circulation: new cabs, developed by Otis, designed to go sideways as well as up and down, permit users to transfer from one bank of elevators to another.

ABOVE Model view, looking west

OPPOSITE, CLOCKWISE FROM LEFT Towers can be doubled to allow for future expansion; model view, to southwest; the section of the Downtown Athletic Club is inverted, replicated, and then conjoined to illustrate the transformation of the typical, bottom-heavy, nine-to-five Manhattan skyscraper into OMA's reconfigured, top-heavy, round-the-clock tower block

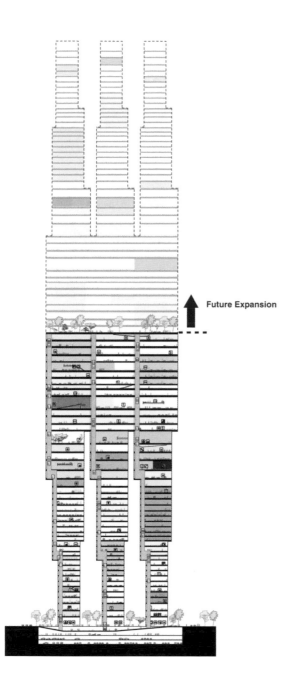

Future Expansion

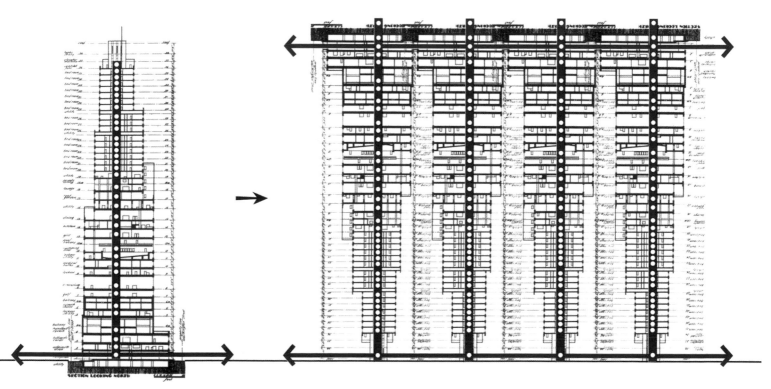

LEFT Collage generated by Rem Koolhaas/OMA for an early meeting of the Downtown Study Group, prior to the focus on West Street: the concept calls for a cultural tower, depicting the built New York work of several prominent architectural practices

OPPOSITE Preceding OMA's inverted tower scheme adopted for the West Street plan, the architects designed intermediate support-services elements, which offer connections to adjacent buildings for shared circulation

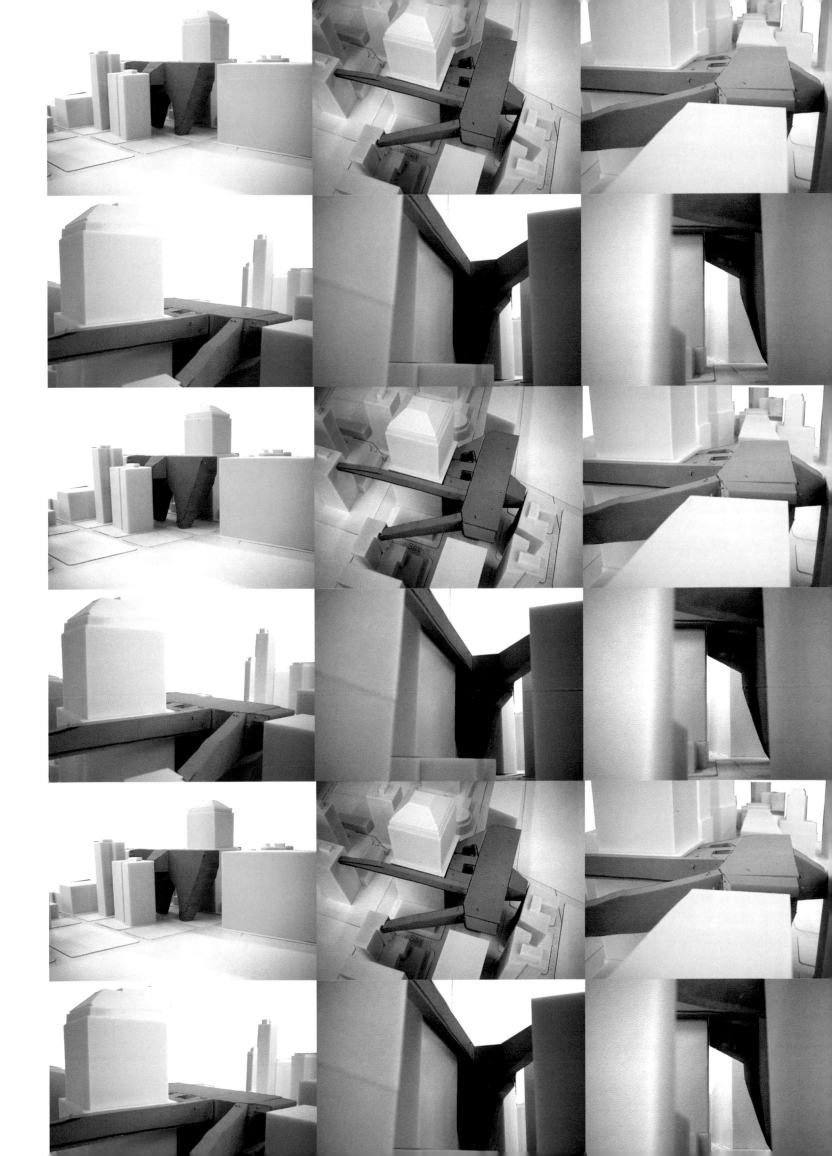

Alexander Gorlin

New York City

Housing

West Street between Rector Place
and Albany Street

OPPOSITE View to south

RIGHT Massing studies

BELOW, LEFT Site plan showing
placement of towers

Fronted by a landscaped square, this apartment tower is split into two formal elements: a lower white brick block set apart for retail and live/work lofts; and an interlocking upper section of residential units with glass curtain walls. A rotated glass cube at ground level provides a light-filled entry lobby to the building. To acknowledge its proximity to Ground Zero, the upper glass block is offset slightly to align with the axes of the World Trade Center tower footprints.

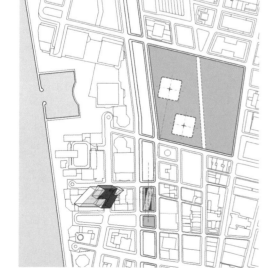

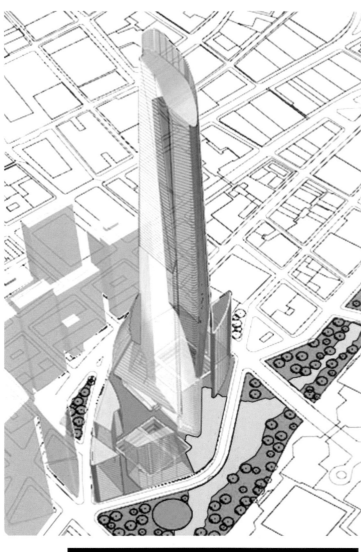

New York Magazine Proposals

September 16, 2002

Organized by Joseph Giovannini, architecture critic for *New York*

CLOCKWISE FROM LEFT Schemes by Carlos Zapata, Wood + Zapata; Zaha Hadid; Thom Mayne, Morphosis; Peter Eisenman; Wolf D. Prix and Helmut Swiczinsky, Coop Himmelb(l)au; William Pedersen, Kohn Pedersen Fox

Like Herbert Muschamp at the *New York Times*, Joseph Giovannini, the architecture critic at *New York* magazine, found that vision was conspicuously lacking in the business-as-usual process for reinventing the World Trade Center in the summer of 2002. The shortlist for the first round of the competition to develop a master plan for Ground Zero was effectively limited to a tight circle of design professionals already established in the region, since the Port Authority of New York and New Jersey and the Lower Manhattan Development Corporation had failed to issue a wide international call for architecture and engineering teams. After the first-round schemes by Beyer Blinder Belle had been rejected at the Town Hall meeting at the Javits Center in July 2002, the city and nation stood empty-handed as the anniversary of the events of September 11, 2001, approached.

To "help establish ideas and open debate about the future of ground zero," Giovannini invited a select group of architects to submit proposals that would be published in *New York* magazine's commemorative issue on September 16, 2002. The architects had only three compressed weeks during August to invent and present a proposal.

Giovannini gave the architects the program as then understood—approximately 11 million square feet of office space—but allowed them to expand the site into air space over West Street, down to the harbor. The program could be mixed, with cultural facilities and residential functions added to the requirement of office space. He stipulated that the footprints of Minoru Yamasaki's World Trade Center towers be respected as the basis of a memorial, but stressed that the whole project necessitated a vision that would honor the dead as well as the living.

By the end of August, the visions that arrived at *New York* magazine represented a wide architectural spectrum, from Zaha Hadid's liquid skyscrapers to Thom Mayne's undulating towers laid on their sides. All the proposals, as Giovannini noted, cultivated an interconnectivity between the interiors of the buildings themselves and explored the three-dimensionality of Manhattan, where the space beneath the asphalt is not necessarily solid ground. Some brought the buildings to the waterfront, and others brought the water into the site. While the schemes were meant to be buildable, feasibility was not the premise, but rather a vehicle for visions to heal the "psychic wounds" of that day.

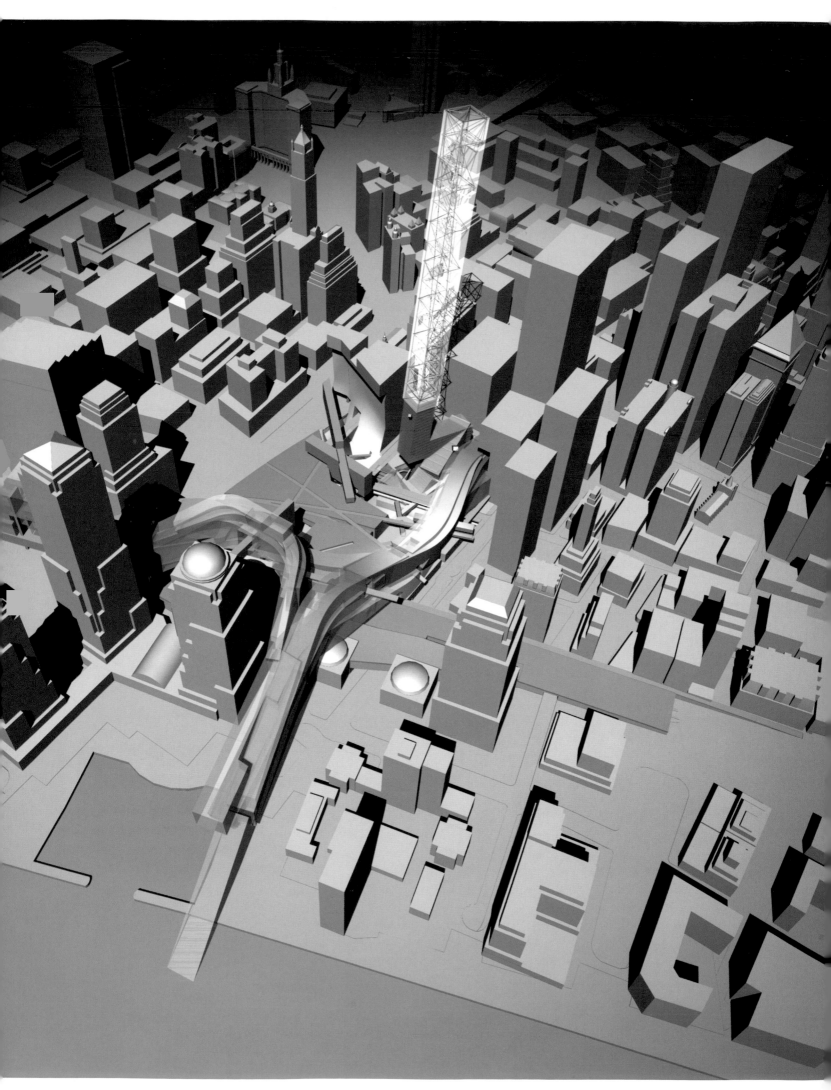

Morphosis

Thom Mayne

Santa Monica, California

Based on an earlier proposal Morphosis exhibited at Max Protetch's Chelsea gallery in fall 2001 (page 175), Thom Mayne's scheme for the former World Trade Center presents a spatial and experiential puzzle—an "affirmation of the living city." Surmounted by a 1,300-foot-tall communications tower to the east (opposite), and descending to a subterranean memorial several stories below grade, the most extensive of these interventions are ribbonlike structures that mark the perimeter of the site to the south, east, and west.

Skirting, intersecting, merging, or piling one atop the other as they spill into the Hudson River, these forms reinterpret the tall office tower, providing much of the commercial office space horizontally. The urban canyons that separate these forms enclose a green space open to the north, and reveal a complex circulation pattern below with transportation facilities, passive recreation space, and retail concourses. Only one of the footprints is left as a void, puncturing the ground plane of the urban park.

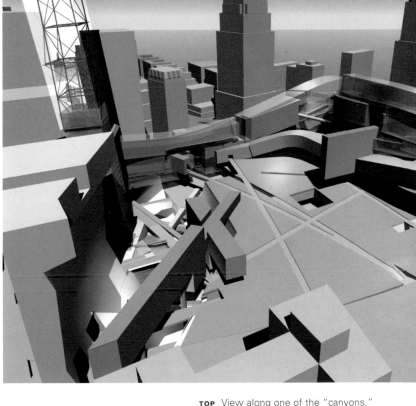

TOP View along one of the "canyons," looking south

ABOVE View to south of memorial park

BELOW Section looking west

OPPOSITE Perspective view east

Coop Himmelb(l)au

Wolf D. Prix, Helmut Swiczinsky

Vienna, Austria

Wolf D. Prix and Helmut Swiczinsky propose a set of three mixed-use towers, arranged in plan to form a right triangle over Ground Zero, with its apex oriented toward the harbor to the south. The bent, 100-story-high towers also act as support piers for an inverted cone-shaped structure containing apartments. Dubbed by Prix and Swiczinsky as an environment for "Skyliving," this suspended structure forms a monumental hourglass with another cone, one that, in turn, protects the footprints of the former Twin Towers within a vaulted, cathedral-like space. An elevated platform flows around this memorial cone and into the spaces between the towers. The configuration creates a plaza for pedestrians above grade and space below for a number of commercial and cultural activities. A raised pedestrian platform hovers above a restored street grid.

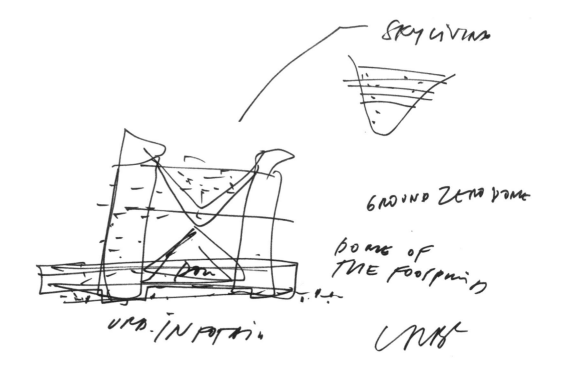

Wood + Zapata

Carlos Zapata

Boston, Massachusetts

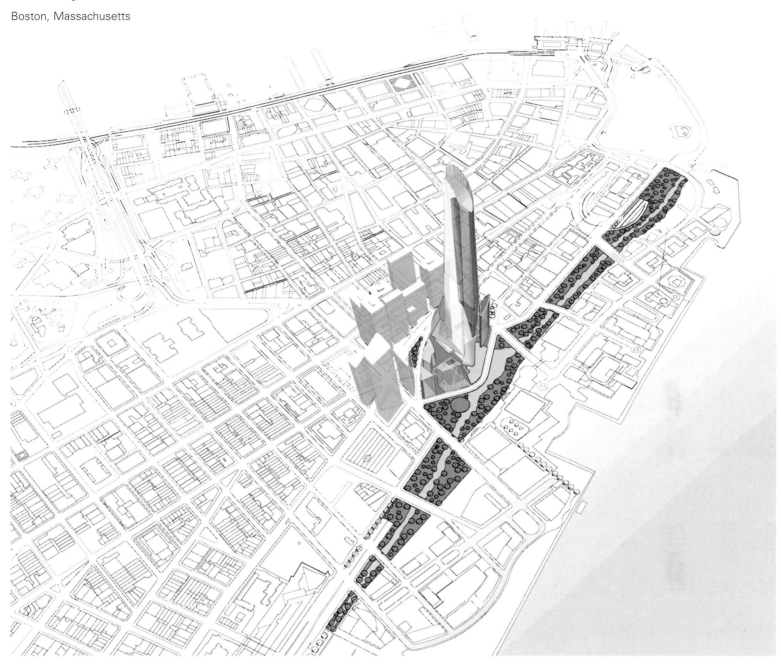

With an iconic tower rising out of a dense mixed-use complex at its base, this design provides 12 million square feet of office, commercial, and residential space as it reconnects parts of the city grid.

As a key element of the project, Carlos Zapata proposes converting West Street into a verdant park bordered by Chambers Street to the north and by the Battery to the south, and arranged along the former waterfront of lower Manhattan before land was reclaimed for Battery Park City. The spine of this park is a flowing tributary of the Hudson River that mimics the original shoreline of Manhattan and forms a pool around the new tower as well as the footprints of the former World Trade Center towers. The footprints themselves are set off by a glass-and-cable structure that allows light to filter below grade.

OPPOSITE View east

ABOVE Axonometric plan of lower Manhattan

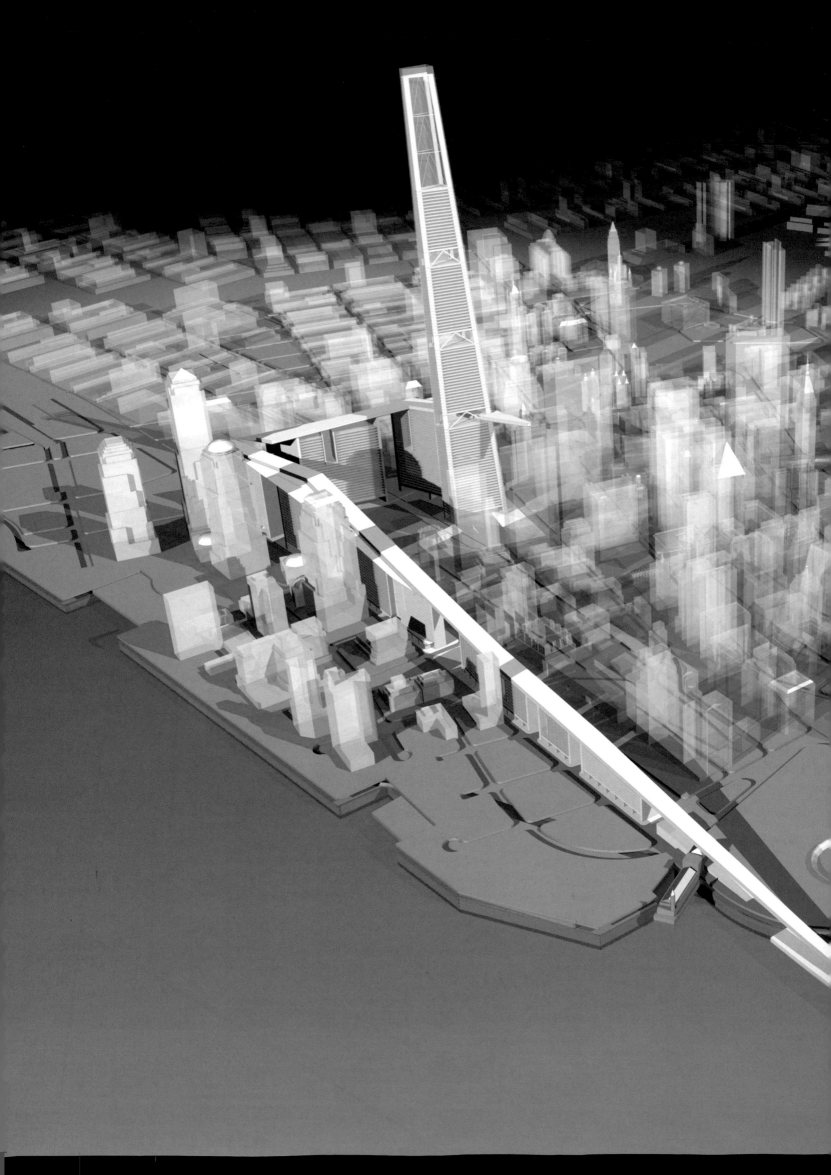

Kohn Pedersen Fox Associates

William Pedersen

New York City

William Pedersen suggests a memorial promenade that evokes the wood-plank deck of the Brooklyn Bridge. Rising at a gentle angle from the southern tip of Manhattan, the "sky promenade" allows pedestrians to walk high above the city. The promenade links earth and sky as it encloses Ground Zero on three sides with a permeable outer wall of mixed-use buildings, defining a memorial precinct for the footprints of the former towers.

The ramp ends in a 2,001-foot-high tower that features an extensive array of wind turbines and solar panels in its upper region to reduce the building's reliance on nonrenewable energy. A perpetual stream of water is pumped from the Hudson River to the top of the tower and is filtered as it is rolls down to the bay, metaphorically cleansing the site.

LEFT Aerial view to the northeast

TOP Sky promenade, looking north

ABOVE Sky promenade, looking south

Eisenman Architects

Peter Eisenman

New York City

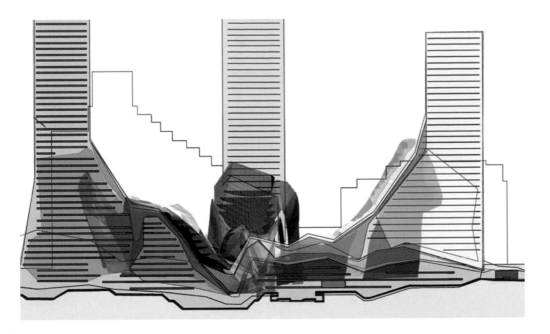

Peter Eisenman proposes a complex that is at once "building, memorial, and landscape" for the 16 acres of the World Trade Center site. In this scheme, the memory of September 11 is given immutable form. Eisenman devises a sequence of orthogonal office high-rises around the still recognizable footprints of the WTC towers. Formally identical at the upper and mid-rise levels, these structures create a familiar skyline of extruded squares. As they descend to meet the ground plane, however, their individual cores fold, collapse, and congeal. Fragmenting into a shared podium, the towers at once emanate from and recede into a common point of origin. As the floor plates expand and intersect within this swirl, the towers achieve programmatic complexity. Within these reconfigured spaces, Eisenman—who consulted with New School University president Bob Kerry—incorporates an urban university, other cultural uses, and a permanent memorial.

OPPOSITE, TOP Section looking north

OPPOSITE, BOTTOM Aerial perspective

ABOVE Perspective looking north

Zaha Hadid Architects

Zaha Hadid

London, England

Ascending to a greater height than the preceding World Trade Center, the twinned, four-part towers that Zaha Hadid and her associate Patrick Schumacher envisioned at the heart of this scheme stand just east of the footprints. Stretched like tubes of molten glass, these two slender forms alternately fuse and glide past one another as they ascend, their mutating floor plates contrasting with the square, repetitive plan of Yamasaki's original buildings. The thinner of the towers is devoted to residential units and the other to office and commercial uses.

At grade, Hadid's proposal recasts the footprints as voids. Below grade, Hadid creates an active substrate of retail, transportation, and cultural uses, with a dense net of circulation woven around the hollow cores.

OPPOSITE Perspective looking
south

BELOW View south revealing
tower structure and circulation
patterns above and below grade

BOTTOM Plan view

Max Protetch Invitational Exhibition

A New World Trade Center: Design Proposals

January 17–February 16, 2002

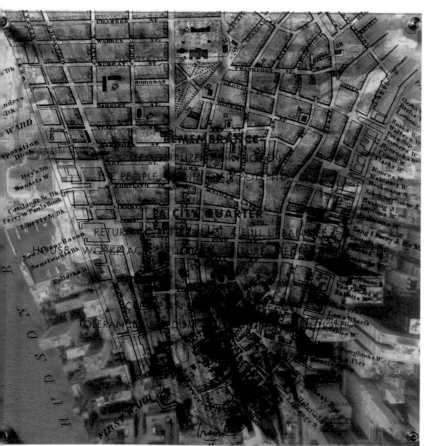

Max Protetch was early in enlisting architects and artists to design a replacement for the ravaged World Trade Center. Some thought too early. A major New York dealer in architecture and art, Protetch began organizing an invitational exhibition of proposals for "A New World Trade Center: Design Proposals" within a month of the shattering occurrence. His invitation was turned down by some architects who felt not enough time had passed to mourn the victims. They wondered if such a gesture smacked of blatant opportunism. Protetch insisted he was doing it out of a sense of optimism. Lower Manhattan would have to be rebuilt, and this was the time for architects to show they had the ideas and the talent to help create a renewed downtown.

Right away Protetch enlisted the help of *Architectural Record* (senior editor Sarah Amelar and editor in chief Robert Ivy) and *Architecture* magazine (editor in chief Reed Kroloff), as well as Aaron Betsky of the Netherlands Architecture Institute, for suggestions of architects to invite. *Architectural Record* decided to help out, after some discussion, with the pragmatic belief that the wheels of politics and economics were probably spinning faster than architecture. If some ideas were not put on the table to improve the World Trade Center site, the rebuilding process would end up being just about money.

While 125 architects and designers were invited, the final number exhibited totaled sixty architectural firms, design teams, and artists. The night the show opened, the participants were stunned by the stampede of spectators and the media. Perhaps it signaled an important stage in the mourning process following September 11. Rather than being subsumed by melancholia, and staying locked into a sense of loss, New Yorkers were redirecting their grief (or displacing it) toward plans for rebuilding.

The Library of Congress found the exhibition noteworthy. As Ford Peatross, curator of architecture, design, and engineering records in the Prints and Photographs Division of the Library of Congress, states, "This collection is a time capsule of current architectural practice. It displays a method of architectural representation, using a range of digital technology that is remarkable." For these reasons, the Library of Congress acquired the material from Protetch for a moderate sum, with the hope it could make the work available to the public.

In comparing the work executed for the show with design done subsequently for the site, the efforts become all the more interesting. Many schemes encapsulate ideas running through later proposals, such as the retention of the footprints of the towers as some form of memorial—often covered by reflecting pools; the idea of burrowing deep into the ground for memorial spaces, and of burying West Street to create pedestrian walks at grade; the use of computer-generated non-Euclidean towers to command the skyline, and the creation of transparent and translucent high-rise structures. A number of architects suggested they were investigating new building techniques and materials, such as carbon fiber structures, lenticular screens, photovoltaic cells, interactive digital design, or electrochromatic glass.

It is interesting to see, for example, how much the Protetch show was a dress rehearsal for Foreign Office Architects and Greg Lynn FORM in a project they collaborated on as part of the United Architects team in the Innovative Design Study sponsored by the Lower Manhattan Development Corporation and the Port Authority of New York and New Jersey. Then, too, it is striking to see the ideas for reclaiming the skyline in a nascent form in Daniel Libeskind's proposal—ideas that would soon be transmuted into the 1,776-foot-high tower for his winning proposal in the Innovative Design Study. By the same token, Thom Mayne's investigation of horizontal forms in the Protetch exhibition eventually would become a commanding "skyscraper" on its side in his entry for Joseph Giovannini's *New York* magazine project.

Some of the submissions to the exhibition present evocative statements about the current moment rather than new proposals. The historic map of New York by Michael Graves is a suggestion to restore the site to its original urban condition. And the drawing by Weiss/Manfredi Architects is a visual expression of silence and reflection, strangely evocative of Balthazar Korab's photograph of the towers in 1978.

This is material from "A New World Trade Center: Design Proposals," an exhibition organized and originally shown at Max Protetch Gallery, New York, and now part of the permanent collection of the Division of Prints and Photographs of the Library of Congress in Washington, D.C. This visual material was documented in a book by Max Protetch, *A New World Trade Center: Design Proposals from Leading Architects Worldwide,* **published in 2002 by ReganBooks (HarperCollins).**

Foreign Office Architects

Farshid Moussavi, Alejandro Zaera-Polo

London, England

For this scheme—eight towers, each 110 stories high, with 10,764 square feet per floor—Foreign Office Architects developed an innovative high-rise form composed of a "bundle" of towers that lend structural support to each other. The towers' facades are constructed of lattice-like tubes that bend to support one another in the same manner as the towers themselves. In each tower, twelve high-speed elevators provide access to all floors; sky lobbies at 36-floor intervals connect to the adjacent towers.

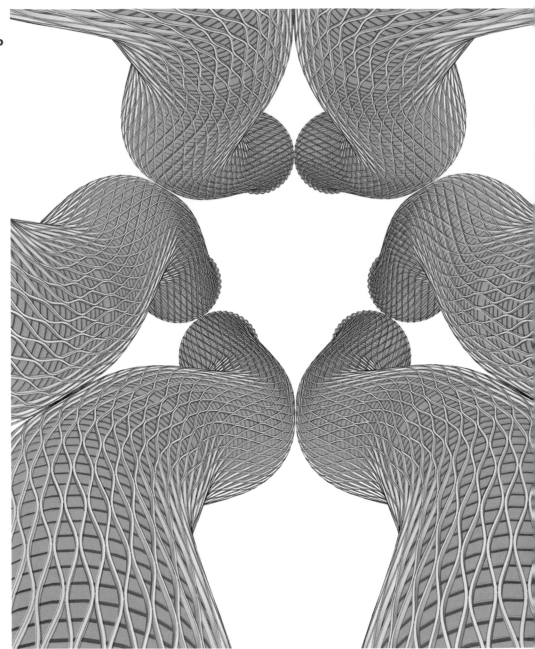

Greg Lynn FORM

Venice, California

Inspired by what he identified as a collapse of the distinctions between military conflict and civilian daily life, Lynn looked to the defensive urban forms of the Middle Ages and the Renaissance. His studies respond to a world in which major architectural projects must assume some potential vulnerability as targets of attack. Lynn's projected forms suggest a mode of defense, in which he sees the architect as a strategist.

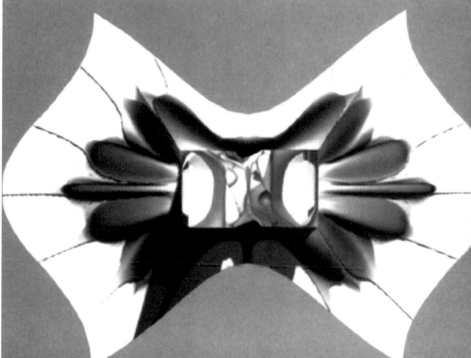

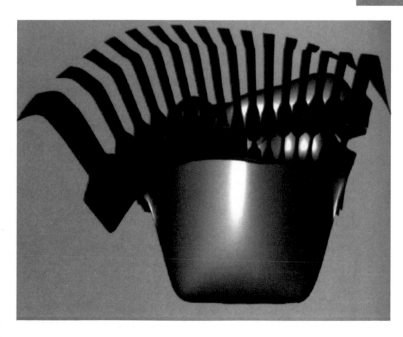

Jakob + MacFarlane

Dominique Jakob, Brendan MacFarlane

Paris, France

Jakob + MacFarlane dedicate the site totally to a memorial as an alternative to creating another facility to accommodate trade. Slender, fingerlike towers are illuminated with messages meant to have global significance.

Office dA

Monica Ponce de Leon, Nader Tehrani

Boston, Massachusetts

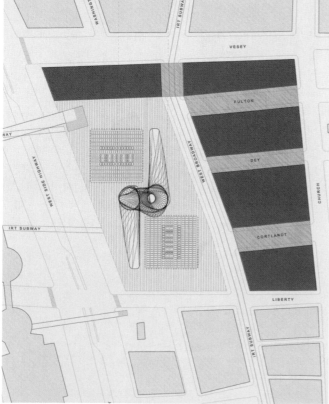

Office dA's scheme emerges from doubts about the validity of the skyscraper type. This ambivalence is expressed in a structure that at its base forms two "trunks" (opposite, left) extending toward differing corners of the site (site plan, left). These then merge into one tall, tapering structure (top left, and above) supported by a triangulated framework that joins at three-floor intervals. Within an undulating mesh skin, there is an array of plans (opposite, right) and sections that show more variation than seen in any traditional skyscraper.

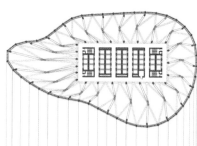

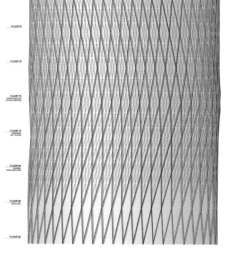

Acconci Studio

Vito Acconci

New York City

This 110-story monolithic structure hovering above the World Financial Center (right) is punctuated by holes, cones, and tubes. While the holes physically embody a new sense of structural vulnerability, the cones function as public spaces, and the tubes as circulation systems. The cones extend through the building as sheltered exterior spaces, while the circulation tubes intersect each other and permeate the building's public and private areas without necessarily providing access to them (sectional rendering, above). The building's interior features "parks," "plazas," and "streets," which function as venues for repose, performance, and gathering.

Oosterhuis.nl

Kas Oosterhuis, Ilona Lénárd

Rotterdam, Netherlands

Driven by the mixture of horror and fascination elicited by video footage of the attacks, the multidisciplinary firm Oosterhuis.nl posits a structure with no fixed form. Instead, the replacement is engaged in a continual process of mutation analogous to the process of destruction and healing. Twelve different configurations (three of which are shown here) project permutations in the structure over the course of twelve months. By proposing a structure that exhibits characteristics of a living organism, the designers have imagined an architecture that can effect an emotional response similar to that realized by many new electronic technologies, though on a much greater scale.

Asymptote
Hani Rashid, Lise Anne Couture
New York City

Designed partly as an homage to the original towers, these "Twin Twins" amplify Minoru Yamasaki's concept for the World Trade Center while exploring new technological, spatial, and digital possibilities of the twenty-first century. The buildings' undulating facades depend on sophisticated technology. Immense apertures admit air and light to the interiors of the vast towers as well as accommodating "sky gardens" with large reflecting pools.

Hariri & Hariri

Gisue Hariri, Mojgan Hariri

New York City

The entire site is devoted to a memorial consisting of eleven towers approximating the monumental scale of the original ones. However, the functions of these towers are limited to providing circulation to observation decks, as well as accommodating mechanical services. The towers are connected by elevated "free-form" structures containing facilities for the New York Stock Exchange and a World Culture Museum. A "smart skin" enveloping the towers displays information on their interiors and exteriors, and features a system of sprinklers and mist releasers that would allow the towers to "weep" during a proposed annual event on September 11.

Tom Kovac

Melbourne, Australia

Depending on digital technology to create form out of data drawn from the physical conditions of the site, this scheme begins with a representation of the site's connections as an "efficiency web." Kovac then introduces data pertaining to pedestrian traffic patterns, this time represented in tubular forms whose thickness corresponds to the data from which they were generated. Layers of information are added in this way, culminating in the introduction of spheres formed from the spatial volumes of the original towers. An envelope for these forms is derived from topological studies of Manhattan.

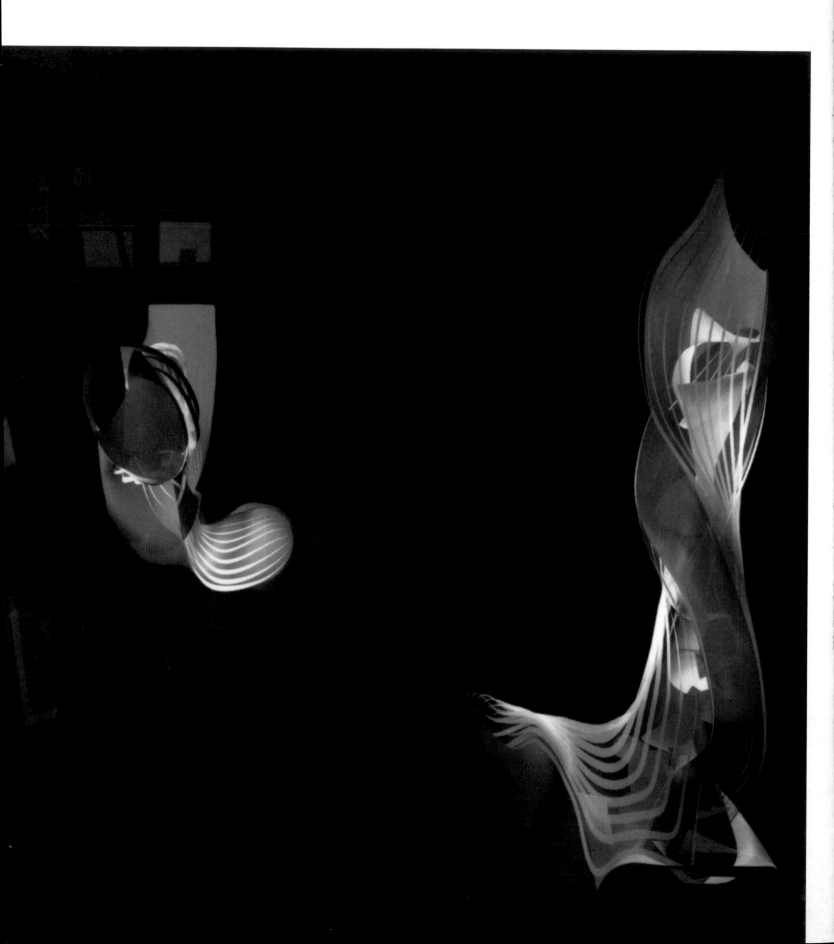

Krueck & Sexton

Ron Krueck

Chicago, Illinois

The footprints of the original towers are marked by circular glass planes etched with the victims' names, with a shallow layer of water washing over them. One of the fragments of the original north tower is retained as a monumental ruin, while the new tower's flexible and lightweight structure supports a mutable and colorful skin expressing vitality and strength.

Kennedy & Violich

Sheila Kennedy, Frano Violich

Boston, Massachusetts

Kennedy & Violich emphasizes creating a dense urban fabric while respecting the primacy of the original towers. The towers' footprints remain as voids within a network of more modestly scaled buildings, and the memorial takes the form of a tower of panels corresponding to the number of victims. The facade of the memorial, clad in a reflective and flexible material, wraps around a free-standing structure; the space between allows public gatherings (opposite, top). The structure itself could be used for a Nobel Peace Center, the architects suggest. A waterway (above) extends from the site to the Hudson River, giving access to a transportation hub for ferry and rail service.

Zaha Hadid

London, England

Hadid's proposal emerges from an interrogation of the nature of organization and aesthetics in the contemporary urban environment, as well as from the assumption that the traditional skyscraper type is no longer a valid response to the commercial demands of the twenty-first century. The result is what Hadid calls an "entity," rather than a building, which functions like a city in microcosm, with the potential for evolution in a manner similar to the larger cityscape.

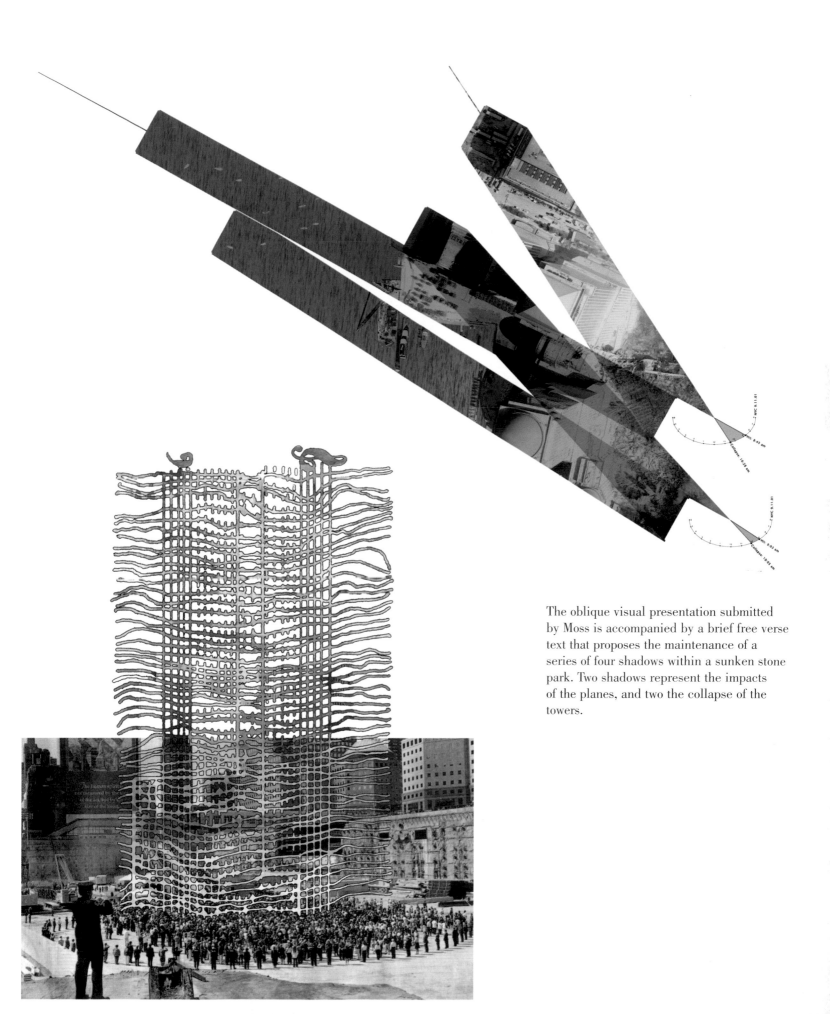

Eric Owen Moss

Culver City, California

The oblique visual presentation submitted by Moss is accompanied by a brief free verse text that proposes the maintenance of a series of four shadows within a sunken stone park. Two shadows represent the impacts of the planes, and two the collapse of the towers.

Libeskind's scheme begins with the proposition that the site's original commercial purpose is no longer sufficient after the events of September 11, 2001. Rather, Libeskind suggests, any construction on the site—whether it is a high-rise structure, as in his presentation, or any other building form—must defer to the area's new function as a place for remembrance. Libeskind's response moves beyond the creation of a memorial to address the magnitude of the attacks' impact on the city.

Preston Scott Cohen with K+D Lab

Harvard Design School

Cambridge, Massachusetts

Memorial space, a park, and areas for commercial use are designed to reconnect the site to the Financial District. Accordingly, a stretch of West Street has been recessed below grade to allow pedestrian streets overhead. The memorial space is conceived as a combination of makeshift shrines and commemorative sculptures as well as pavers placed at the location of the original towers. Extremely slender towers accommodate various corporate, retail, and residential needs.

1100 Architect

David Piscuskas, Juergen Riehm

New York City

A vertical structure occupies the space between the footprints of the original World Trade Center towers and rises to their full height, while reflecting pools occupy the footprints themselves. Two planes extending from the main structure are clad in large panels of glass. A plaza is created over a portion of West Street—which is submerged below ground—and two buildings, fifty to sixty stories high, are located at the north and east sides of the site.

Raimund Abraham

New York City

Central to Abraham's proposal are the times of the attacks and the collapse of the towers—8:46, 9:02, 9:59, and 10:28 A.M.—which are commemorated by three monolithic concrete slabs. They offer no habitable space, but are bisected at angles that are oriented to the morning sun as a natural memorial to the events of September 11, 2001. The slabs are 880 feet long, 110 feet wide, 550 feet tall, and are placed 110 feet apart. The angled slices through the slabs are 33 feet wide and run the full height of the slabs.

Steven Holl

New York City

Holl's proposal calls for a floating memorial hall connected to a new bridge over West Street. The bridge leads to a new "folded street" structure (middle and right), a tower where various commercial and cultural amenities are located. The glass-surfaced tower, constructed of large-scale trusses, supports a series of observation decks (bottom). Two reflecting pools occupy the footprints of the original towers, with glass "lenses" distributing light to spaces beneath the pools.

LOT-EK

Ada Tolla, Giuseppe Lignano

New York City

Approaching the World Trade Center site as a contemporary archaeological ruin, LOT-EK has retained the 70-foot-deep depression of the site, with its void four city blocks in size, and located eight towers along one edge. The facades appear to be "severed," exposing their concrete skeletons. The towers' heights can vary and expand separately, to as much as one hundred stories. The streets that ran east to west before the World Trade Center was built are resurrected as pedestrian bridges across the void. The firm's favored vocabulary of modified containers appear as spatial elements, supported here by a light structural frame.

Winka Dubbeldam

Archi-Tectonics

New York City

This innovative scheme proposes "Flex-City," an interactive environment, which, according to changes in various data, can produce eighty-one scenarios for downtown Manhattan. The result of this level of interactivity is the introduction of new building typologies to the area as well as Dubbeldam's concepts of "Flex Space" (accommodating education, medical facilities, and commerce) and "Green Flex" (parks, tree-lined streets, etc.). Flex-City's goal is to create an urban model sensitive to shifts in such factors as economic stability and local politics, and accommodating overlapping "live-work-play-learn zones" amenable to constant regeneration.

Marwan Al-Sayed

Phoenix, Arizona

Five slender towers change appearance with variations in color from season to season, on holidays, or even at the whim of an invited artist. The towers' structure anticipates developments in carbon fiber systems, and fiber optics allow it to be extraordinarily light and strong, plus distribute sunlight throughout the interior spaces. These technologies also facilitate the shifts in the towers' appearance. By positioning the towers at the site's perimeter, Al-Sayed frees space for an elevated, grass-covered plaza, which is approached from the street level on the north and south by two monumental sets of stairs.

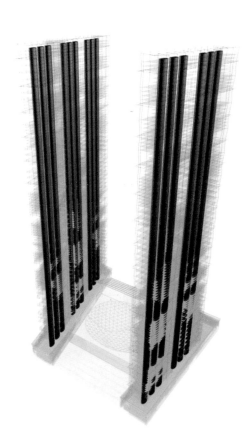

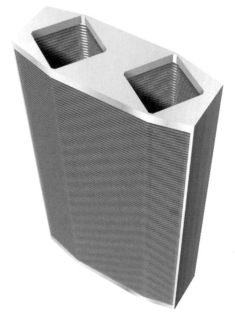

Nathan McRae

Keenen/Riley

New York City

Two voids in the form of the original towers occupy the center of this wide structure. The facade of the new tower is largely transparent, so that the outlines of the towering voids are legible from the exterior. The voids are illuminated at night, providing even greater legibility, and are accessible at ground level as memorial space.

Daniel Kaplan

Fox & Fowle

New York City

A major transportation hub—on a scale approaching Grand Central Terminal—and an urban park—created by sinking a portion of West Street below ground—link the World Trade Center site to the surrounding urban context. The rest of the complex includes multiuse loft buildings ranging from thirty to forty stories, an eighty-story tower, and cultural buildings adjacent to a partially enclosed memorial space. The footprints of the original towers remain vacant as a reminder of the event.

Carlos Brillembourg

New York City

Inspired by what he perceived to be the utopian spirit behind the construction of the World Trade Center, Brillembourg created a scheme that focuses on the towers' role as a symbolic gateway. He repeats the silhouette of the original towers, while opening up their cores. Therefore the new towers feature a 40 percent increase in window coverage. In addition, Brillembourg proposes that some of the space be reserved for commercial functions and some for residential use, particularly as subsidized housing for artists and writers.

Gluckman Mayner Architects

**Richard Gluckman and
Srdjan Javonovic Weiss**

New York City

Gluckman Mayner Architects revives the silhouettes of the original towers, but provide the facades with skins that change with a combination of glass and digital media. More specifically, electrochromatic glass alters the facades' color and level of opacity, and lenticular screens and holography create dynamic surfaces. The space behind these surfaces accommodates all of the programmatic requirements for the site, including residential, commercial, and memorial functions.

Alexander Gorlin Architects

Alexander Gorlin, Brendan Cotter

New York City

Inspired by the Hindu concept of temporal reality being a dream in the mind of the deity Vishnu, Alexander Gorlin and Brendan Cotter concentrated on the ephemeral nature of life and art to create two structures that occupy the footprints of the original World Trade Center towers. The structures are each 110 feet high, a symbolic compression of the towers' 110 stories, and their facades are outfitted with a liquid crystal display of the victims' names. A transparent ground plane reveals the ruins of the towers' foundations and the surrounding transportation lines.

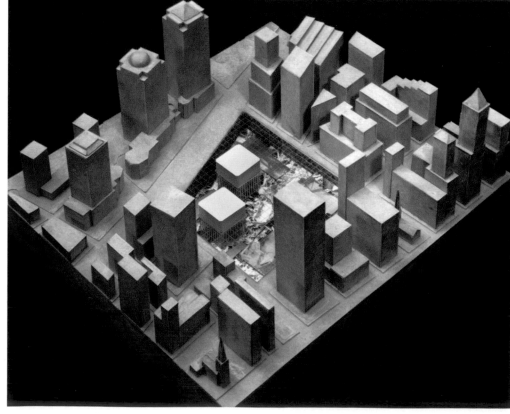

Hugh Hardy

Hardy Holzman Pfeiffer

New York City

In his statement accompanying his sketches of a new New York skyline, Hardy expressed an ambivalent attitude toward the World Trade Center towers. On the one hand he considered them to be the culmination of an era of towering boxes, while on the other he acknowledged that their absence had a diminishing effect on the skyline. His proposal is a rallying cry to find in the aftermath of tragedy the opportunity to renew the entire profile of the city by introducing a greater variety of architecture.

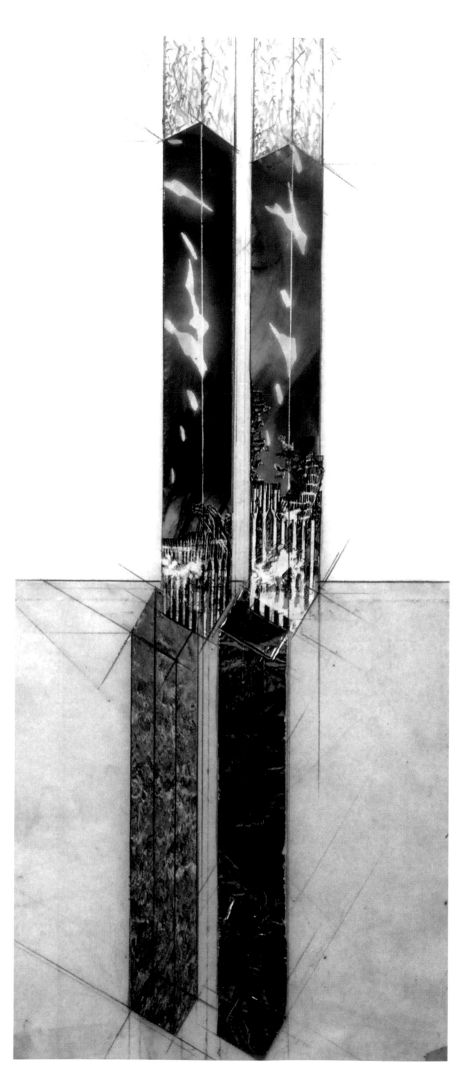

Barbara Stauffacher Solomon
& Nellie King Solomon

San Francisco, California

Two new steel and mirrored glass towers rise higher than the original towers, while below ground two memorials under the original towers' footprints reach a depth of 110 stories, the height of the original towers. One of these deep sunken memorials is filled with water, while the other is faced with a mirrored surface to achieve a kaleidoscope effect, and each are illuminated from their depths.

Samuel Mockbee

Canton, Mississippi

Conceived while Mockbee was hospitalized during his final hours of life, this scheme places a memorial chapel and cultural center along with a reflecting pool 911 feet below ground. This subterranean series of spaces is accessible via elevators and a spiral walkway, a descent that carries the potential for much symbolic power, particularly in light of the architect's own proximity to mortality. Above ground, two new towers rise to greater heights than the original towers, and are visible from the depths of the memorial below.

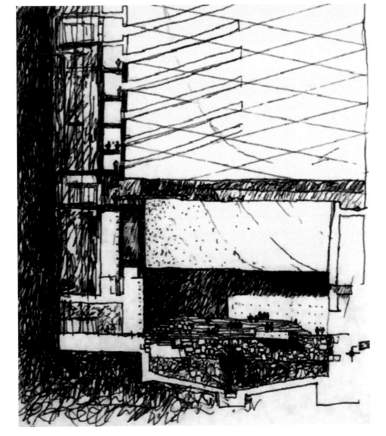

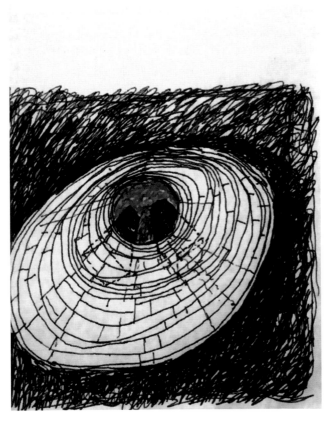

Tod Williams Billie Tsien

New York City

Mehrdad Yazdani

Los Angeles, California

Two drawings comprise this proposal: The first depicts a cluster of trees, and the architects' accompanying statement suggests the possibility of space below ground extending in the manner of a system of roots. The second drawing (below) shows a ring of tall towers along the edge of the site, again hinting at treelike forms, this time creating a clearing at the site's center. The ring of towers is connected by a thickly banded structure that contains a public gathering space.

A mixed-use structure occupies the center of the site while still retaining the footprints of the original towers as a memorial where twin gardens offer space for reflection and gathering. The new structure functions as a "center for the humanities," accommodating a museum, a library, and a conference center, and is complemented by a series of high-rise towers containing office space. A variety of forms is prescribed to respond to the more rigid profiles of the surrounding buildings, and to mark the site as being unique within the city's fabric.

RoTo Architects

Michael Rotondi, Clark Stevens

Los Angeles, California

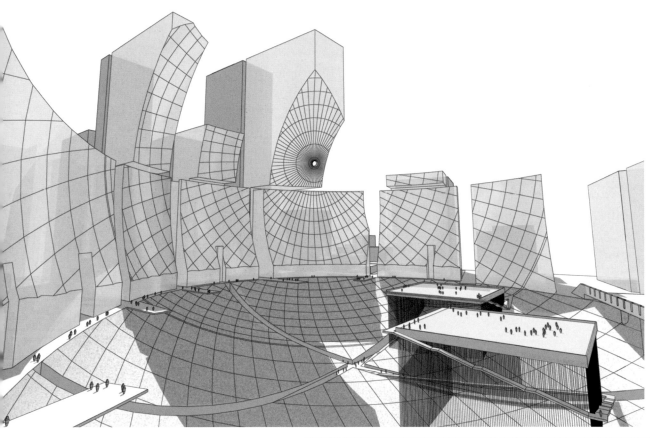

The footprints of the original towers become the site of two lawns extruded from a monumental elliptical basin. The lawns are supported by columns, whose number corresponds to that of the victims. New construction will surround the basin, which suggests the form of an open palm, to provide 11 million square feet of usable space. An aperture set into one of the new buildings is oriented to the sun so that light will pass through it annually on September 11, at 8:46 A.M. Four tall buildings along the basin's edge, approximating the "fingers" of the open palm, will comprise a proposed World Citizens Conference Center, dedicated to education and open dialogue.

Ben Nicholson

Chicago, Illinois

Nicholson conceived this proposal as part of a satire he wrote called *The World: Who Gets It and Who Wants It?*, which, according to Nicholson, presents "a world order in which a new World Trade Center could relax its guard against further assault." In this version of the post–September 11 world, the commercial functions of the World Trade Center have been shifted to Newark, New Jersey. The site of the original towers is now occupied by a series labyrinths and a 500-foot-deep shaft containing an enormous ball of gold bullion, which functions as a pilgrimage destination, and is described as a frenzy of greed reminiscent of a scene painted by Hieronymus Bosch.

Michael Sorkin Studio

New York City

In this comprehensive urban redevelopment plan, an earth berm surrounds the site with a public viewing platform, creating a modest memorial space. West Street is sunken below ground to eliminate through traffic and provide room for a "seam" of green space to help unify the urban fabric of lower Manhattan. A ferry terminal at the World Financial Center's yacht harbor is linked to PATH and subway lines. The scheme is dependent upon the redistribution of office space to various other centers around the city (Jamaica, Flushing, the Bronx Hub) and pier construction on lower Manhattan's east side.

Hodgetts + Fung Design Associates

Craig Hodgetts, Ming Fung

Culver City, California

Hodgetts + Fung name their proposal for the World Trade Center site One World Plaza, which was developed in conjunction with a proposal for a Museum of the Family of Man. The entire site is reserved for the plaza, composed of a circular lawn 600 feet in diameter, two reflecting pools occupying the footprints of the towers, and a grove of trees

situated where the towers' shadows were cast on the morning of the attacks. Buildings with 8 to 10 million square feet of office space are placed along the periphery of the site (below), while the museum is located under the plaza (section, bottom).

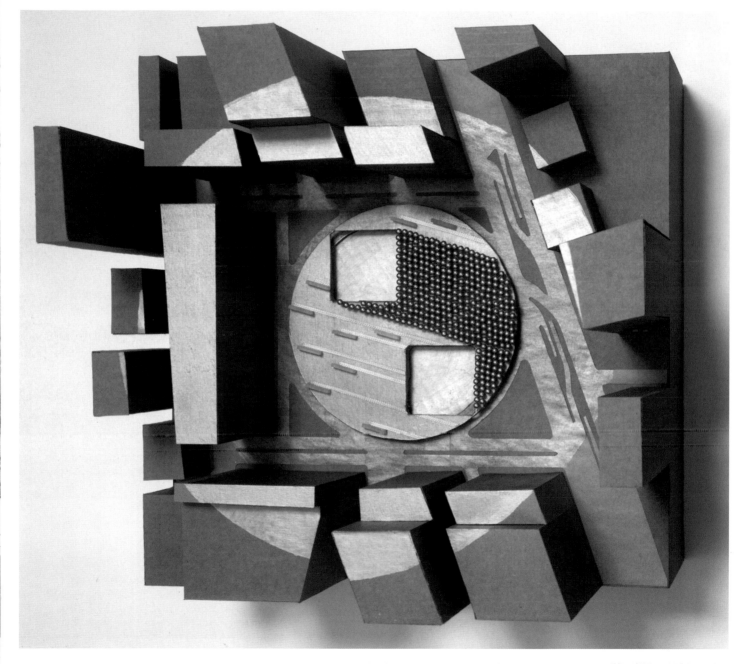

Thom Mayne
base on whic
one end. Vert
emphasis on
eration of str
umes suggest
the site. The
and multiplic
first-century
here have bec
original exhib

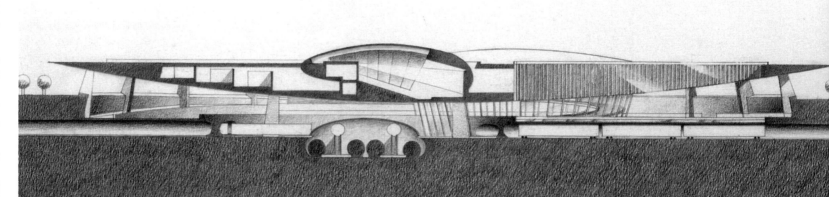

Shigeru Ban

Tokyo, Japan

Ban's response to the events of September 11 came in the form of a modest, temporary memorial inspired by his experiences building his "Paper Church" after the 1995 earthquake in Kobe, Japan. Like the church, Ban's memorial makes use of paper tubes for its structure. In his statement accompanying the proposal, Ban emphasizes that his design is a deliberate alternative to the introduction of another high-rise structure on the site.

Brad Cloepfil

Allied Works Architecture

Seattle, Washington

A labyrinth of buildings contains within its confines a series of spaces for gathering and reflection. A public square at ground level reconnects the site to the surrounding urban fabric, while "streets" on the third and tenth floors, and the rooflike structure over nearly the entire site create additional public space. The proposal's central conceit is what the architect calls a "room for memory," an empty space high above ground level devoted to honoring the victims.

Hans Hollein

Vienna, Austria

Hollein proposes to rebuild the World Trade Center towers, connecting them with a horizontal structure that appears to hover above them (below). Based in part on ideas for adding horizontal extensions to Manhattan's vertical skyline that Hollein began to develop in the early 1960s (bottom), the new horizontal structure contains a memorial to victims of terrorism around the globe, plus an information center on the fight against terrorism.

Coop Himmelb(l)au

Wolf D. Prix, Helmut Swiczinsky

Vienna, Austria

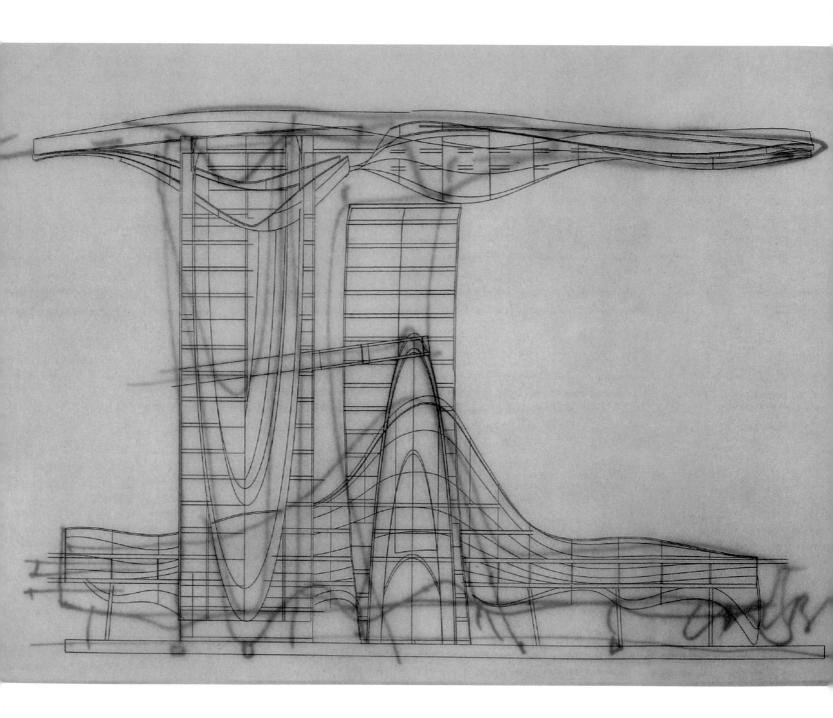

By upending the traditional skyscraper form, Coop Himmelb(l)au creates "reversed towers." The forms, technology, and multiple functions of the structures are meant to bring a renewed focus and sense of optimism to lower Manhattan.

Paolo Soleri

Mayer, Arizona

This fanciful proposal offers a "secular cathedral" in the form of a cylindrical tower. It is outfitted with a series of slides capable of evacuating the structure in approximately twenty minutes. Magnetically powered modes of conveyance are specified, which in addition to elevators and escalators would include exterior gondolas. The tower's lower floors are devoted to spaces for gathering and entertainment, while the upper forty to fifty stories accommodate commercial activity and social institutions.

The slide emergency evaluation proposition is part of the child's play. Fun overlaid upon incipient tragedy. Fun running on the celebratory umbrella of city life. The city as it is (the ring) and the city as it could become, the center.

SITE

James Wines

New York City

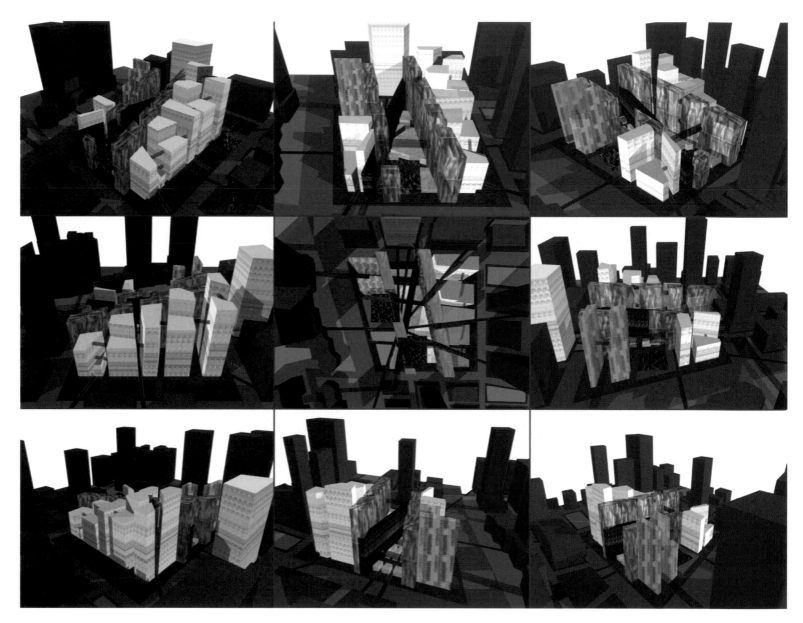

A plan for a memorial garden emphasizes sustainable architecture and reinstates all the streets in the city's grid, which had disappeared with the construction of the World Trade Center. Gone is the super-skyscraper: in its place are ten- to thirty-story buildings designed by a variety of architects. In the footprints of the two towers are dense clusters of arborvitae trees. The gardens are dedicated to the members of the fire department, police department, and the Port Authority who lost their lives on September 11, while in an area below street level a water wall structure bears all the victims' names.

Eytan Kaufman Design and Development

New York City

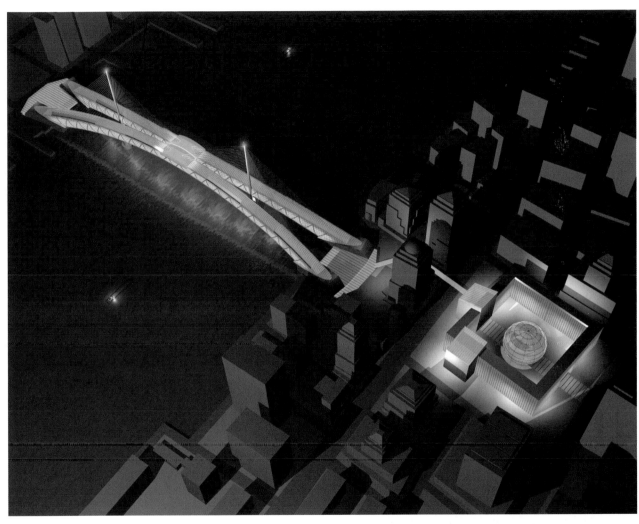

Two separate components comprise this proposal. The first, a World Forum at the World Trade Center site, is marked by a dome whose interior surface displays projections of information on global developments. Buildings at the periphery of the plaza accommodate cultural and commercial requirements, and rise no higher than twelve stories. The second component, a World Bridge, extends one mile across the Hudson River to Jersey City. It contains a park/promenade, retail and office space, a hotel, and theaters and galleries, totaling approximately 6 million square feet.

Mel Chin

Burnsville, North Carolina

A Tribute in Light

John Bennett, Gustavo Bonevardi, Richard Nash-Gould, Julian LaVerdiere, Paul Myoda

New York City

A horizontal modular structure, suspended 72 feet above the streets of New York, is supported by its neighboring buildings. With such features as a fiber-optic canopy, the platform in turn supplies water, power, and information as a systemic solution to development. Included in the project are work and leisure spaces that can shift around on a grid.

The team of designers responsible for the Tribute in Light conceived the project as a temporary installation of twin beacons of light emanating from lower Manhattan as a memorial to the victims, an acknowledgment of the efforts of the city's rescue workers, and a source of hope and strength to all New Yorkers. The project was realized on March 11, 2002, and the Tribute in Light illuminated the night sky for millions around the metropolitan area for the following month.

A. OP POWER STATION

Organo-pneumatic, expiremental, light-weight, power-generating station has expanding and contracting solar cell skin.

B. WORK MODULES

Office/Studios come in many varieties: Independent Personal Models (IPM) or Interlocking Modular Types (IMT)

C. LP SCAPES

Diverse plantings on landscape platforms go where "green" is desired.

D. CAMOCANOPY

A fiber optic network transmits the sky above to the street below.

E. The GRID

Modular support system features CPU-enhanced "smart" structural construction. Power, water, data, organics, and a reactive neural capacity flow through it like living systems.

F. MOBILE COMPOSTING STATION

All GRID wastes treated with bio/aquatic processes.

Proposals as Commentary

An array of entries to the Max Protetch exhibition functioned more as commentaries than as actual solutions to a problem. Wrapping a skyscraper in a flag as Morris Adjmi has done, or filling the footprints with water and planting trees around them, as Frei Otto proposed, were only two such responses. Iñigo Manglano-Ovalle's sound sculpture, or Marjetica Potrč's idea for making use of renewable energy sources represent alternative artistic responses. Will Alsop's suggestion that new towers, twice the height of the World Trade Center, should be erected, with one used for offices, the other empty, offers a physical and metaphysical architectural idea. Quite different in character is the device architects Jared Della Valle and Andrew Bernheimer came up with. They proposed creating an assemblage of blocks that could be used by varied community groups in deciding and programming the redesign of downtown. Stan Allen and James Corner of Field Operations suggested an off-site earthwork at Fresh Kills, Staten Island, since this was the place where investigators searched through the debris for the missing in the days after September 11.

TOP
Morris Adjmi
New York City

ABOVE
Frei Otto
Stuttgart, Germany

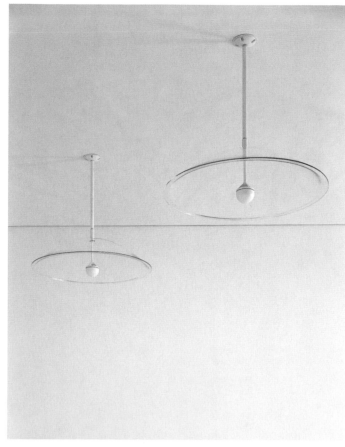

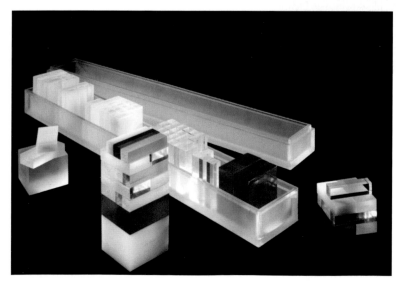

185

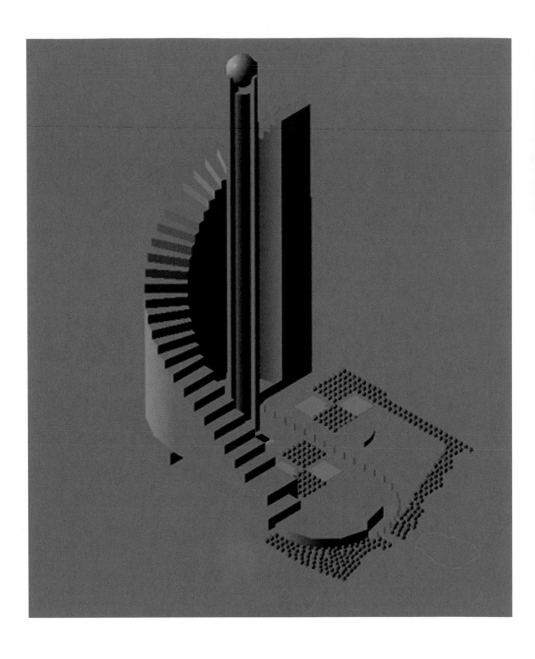

Independent Submissions

**Self-Generated Proposals and
Unpremiated Competition Entries**

September 2001–March 2004

S ince fall 2001, countless architects and designers have
submitted schemes to various official agencies and press
outlets, including *Architectural Record*. In some instances
the schemes adhere to the parameters established by the
Lower Manhattan Development Corporation for its Innovative
Design Study competition for the site's master plan, or for the
memorial competition. In other cases, the architects and designers choose to critique these constraints, or to offer their own
independent proposals.

The following pages show both schemes encompassing the
entire 16-acre site or only for the memorial (usually on the
4.7-acre site at the former World Trade Center footprints).
A cluster of memorial schemes were submitted to the memorial
competition, but were not among the eight finalists. One, however, designed by Fred Bernstein, was initially included as a
finalist (the ninth) until the judges discovered that Bernstein's
scheme had to be disqualified on a technicality. Bernstein had
designed a memorial, Twin Piers, before the competition, and
posted it on his Web site. When the competition was
announced, he saw his scheme fell outside the guidelines, so
he submitted a second one. However, participants were only
allowed to submit one entry. A friend of Bernstein's thought the

OPPOSITE WTC site scheme, Stuart Ohlson of Ohlson Lavoie, Denver, Colorado

RIGHT Memorial scheme, John David Rulon, Rutherford, California

Twin Piers scheme had merit and, with Bernstein's permission, submitted it under his name. But when the judges decided on the scheme, it soon was revealed that Bernstein was the designer, and he was no longer in the running.

Technicalities that rule against imaginative entries are the lore of architectural history: Le Corbusier's League of Nations scheme (1927) being disqualified because he used India ink instead of the required Chinese ink is a famous one. While Fred Bernstein (an architectural writer, not an architect) may not achieve the same sort of martyrdom, his scheme nevertheless proved to be distinct from the finalists who followed the rules.

The case also illustrates the appeal of this memorial as a design problem for those who are not necessarily designers. For that reason, it is interesting to note that Arthur Carter, the publisher of a well-known weekly newspaper, the *New York Observer*, and a sculptor on the side, came up with a scheme for a memorial, aided by Centerbrook Architects.

Critic and architect Michael Sorkin has submitted proposals both for the site and for the memorial, and has even published them in a book, *Starting from Zero: Reconstructing Downtown New*

York (2003). The various schemes presented on the following pages demonstrate a range of drawing styles as well as proposals from Sorkin.

Richard Dattner, a New York City architect who has designed P.S. 234 near Battery Park City and the World Trade Center, came up with a torqued (or rotated) twin tower design early—September 17, 2001. He modified his concept and sent his proposal to Larry Silverstein, the developer for the site, who gave it to David Childs of SOM, his architect. Freedom Tower's affinity to Dattner's concept is not so close that they need to talk about intellectual property rights. It, as well as others on these pages, demonstrates that a good idea can have many manifestations, appearing and reappearing, like some sort of genetic strain, with its recombinant DNA. Indeed, as shown by the WTC site scheme by Stuart Ohlson of Ohlson Lavoie, or the memorial by John David Rulon, spiral and stepped motifs from older cultures or natural science continue to inspire.

MEMORIAL

Ellsworth Kelly

Chatham, New York

The seemingly simple imposition of a green space into an aerial photograph of the site represents artist Ellsworth Kelly's call for a direct spiritual connection to the events of September 11. Rather than filling the site with the distracting effects of new construction, and the processes behind its selection, this collage suggests that the more appropriate response to overwhelming tragedy is silence. Published in the *New York Times*, August 31, 2003, the proposal is now part of the Whitney Museum of American Art's permanent collection.

Ellsworth Kelly
Ground Zero, 2003
8 x 12 inches (20.3 x 32.4 cm)
Whitney Museum of American Art, gift of the artist
and anonymous donor
© Ellsworth Kelly

Tadao Ando

Tokyo, Japan

First seen around the end of 2001, Tadao Ando's elegantly austere proposal calls for the construction of a circular tomb over the major part of the site, which is intended for mourning and reflection. The tomb's radius, approximately one thirty-thousandth the radius of the earth, rises as a shallow dome to a height of about 100 feet above ground level.

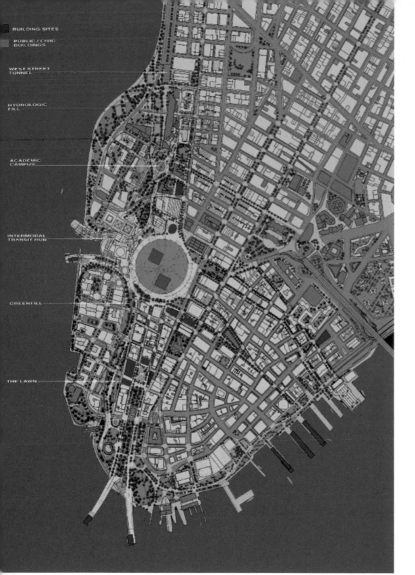

Michael Sorkin Studio

New York City

Lower Manhattan Plan

In November 2001, Michael Sorkin developed this comprehensive plan (left) for lower Manhattan. Still of the opinion that it would be premature to address the specific requirements of Ground Zero, Sorkin and his team moved beyond the site to propose a series of large-scale interventions, including the placement of several traffic arteries below ground to create green space at street level, plus the creation of an urban campus for multiple educational institutions and a major transportation hub. Also proposed is the redistribution of many of the functions of the original site to outlying neighborhoods throughout the city.

World Peace Dome

In September 2002, as an alternative to introducing yet another tall tower to the site, Sorkin proposed an immense dome (right), whose form is legible as a place for gathering, as well as being a prominent object in the skyline. Within the dome are gardens, a major transportation hub, and crescent-shaped towers, which are to accommodate cultural institutions and nongovernmental organizations working toward global peace.

The Lotus

By October 2002, the enclosure of the World Peace Dome had been removed (below), and this second iteration of the structures within the dome took shape. Free of the constraints of the dome, buildings become sinuous, tendril-like towers, complemented by space devoted to cultural institutions below ground. Additionally, a transport concourse connects the transit lines that meet at the site to those lines located to the east. Finally, a major cultural venue occupies the rebuilt block south of Dey Street.

WTC SITE

Michael Sorkin Studio

New York City

The Lotus refined scheme

Various computer-aided renderings represent a significant development from the original drawings. While the first hand-drawn treatments reflect much of Sorkin's initial ambivalence around future construction on the site, these computer drawings show a later commitment to the exploration of structural viability and formal refinement. Of particular note is the section (opposite, bottom), which shows the considerable space provided below grade for cultural and institutional functions.

Michael Sorkin Studio

New York City

Back to Zero

Conceived in April 2003, this scheme reserves the site for a public park, pushing all commercial, residential, and cultural functions to the site's periphery. Within the immense green space, two reflecting pools occupy the footprints of the original towers. The pools' transparent glazed floors serve as the ceiling of a memorial hall and chapel below ground. In the harbor, replicas of the original towers, built at 1:10 scale, stand as beacons.

Bernard Tschumi

New York City

In the year following the attack on the World Trade Center, architect Bernard Tschumi, then dean of Columbia University's Graduate School of Architecture, Planning, and Preservation, helped organize seminars, studios, and a symposium devoted to Ground Zero. On his own, Tschumi worked on a "counter-project" to the Lower Manhattan Development Corporation's schemes executed in the summer of 2002. He questioned the context—and not just that of Ground Zero: "The architect does not decide the context; society does . . . the architect may suggest a context and offer it as a choice to a society." The results of these efforts appear in *Tri-Towers of Babel: Questioning Ground Zero* (Columbia Books of Architecture, Columbia University). His "Tri-Towers of Babel" is a complex linked in two places at the middle and separated at the top and bottom. In this form, the scheme can include

both small (30,000 to 35,000 square feet) and large (90,000 to 200,000 square feet) floor plates for programmatic flexibility. Ample access to natural daylight is provided to the interior spaces. Tschumi also points out that the project can be adapted to any context (opposite, top), but, in relation to the World Trade Center site (above and right), one tower could be given over to the memorial and museum, another tower to a hotel and residential complex, while the third could contain commercial office space. The ground plane creates a triangular space for the transit hub, with the remaining area left as outdoor open space. In another version Tschumi shows how the Tri-Towers could be multiplied throughout greater New York City (opposite, bottom).

21st Century City of Eternal Memory

21st Century City of Patriots

21st Century City of Spectacle

21st Century City of Friendship and Brotherhood

Richard Dattner

New York City

In a scheme first proposed in September 2001, architect Richard Dattner designed two structures linked by bridges at three points, which appear as rotated versions of the original World Trade Center towers. The footprints of the original towers are preserved as memorial sites, with landscaped courtyards and fountains. Dattner calls for the towers and other low-rise buildings on the site to be constructed of sustainable materials.

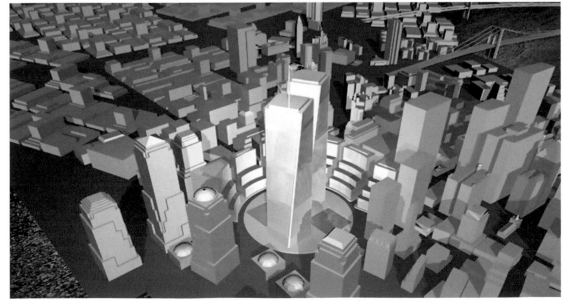

Macrae-Gibson Architects

Gavin Macrae-Gibson

New York City

In Gavin Macrae-Gibson's scheme for the World Trade Center site, developed independently at the time of the Innovative Design Study (fall 2002), a central plaza is surrounded by two concentric rings of new structures. The inner ring is composed of low-rise cultural buildings, the outer ring of office towers and transportation facilities. Trees, whose locations are determined by a map of sites where victims' remains were found, shade the central plaza. The ground rises slightly over the original towers' footprints, with beams of light emitted from each. The center of the north tower is the site of a circular memorial hall rising 80 feet high. The area of the south tower is left solid, with a memorial object at its center.

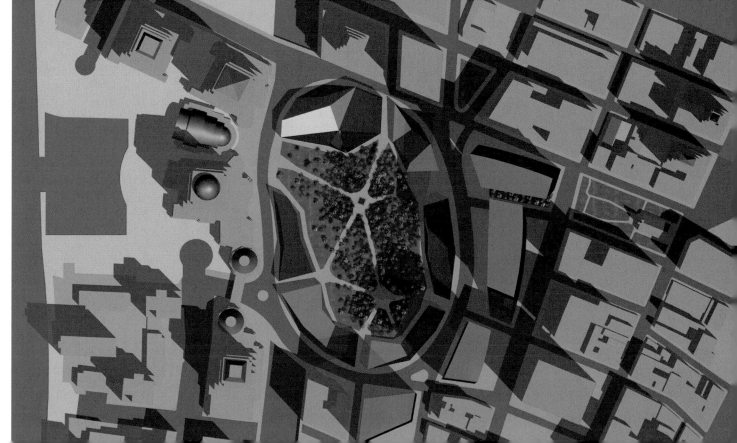

Pierre-Louis Carlier

Paris, France

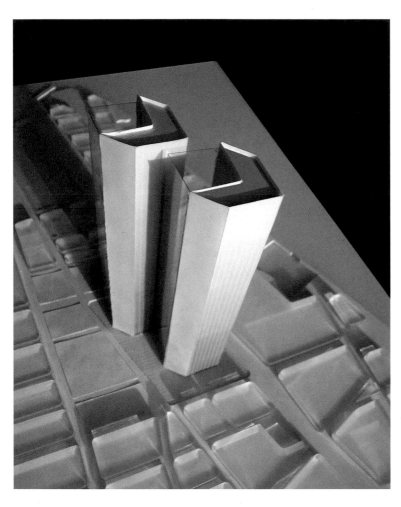

Conceived during the time of the Innovative Design Study (fall 2002), Pierre-Louis Carlier's scheme preserves the volumes of the original towers as negative space, wrapped by new V-shaped towers. Reflecting pools occupy the footprints of the original towers. An interfaith chapel, in the form of a 100-foot cube, sits at the base of the new south tower, and an underground transportation hub is located beneath the stone plaza. Commercial and residential structures fill the remainder of the site in a rehabilitation of the blocks between Vesey and Liberty streets.

Randall Dolph

San Diego, California

During fall 2002, architect Randall Dolph
came up with a scheme where the structural
framework of the new towers preserves the
profiles of the original towers as voids and
accommodates new L-shaped towers. The
footprints of the original towers at the base
of these "megastructures" feature two
translucent, skylit memorials, with 1,000
freestanding columns surrounding each footprint. A multilevel plaza contains smaller
cultural pavilions, gardens, and fountains,
and offers access to the new buildings at
various levels.

west street

MEMORIAL GROUND

UNDERGROUND "BATHTUB"

WTC SITE

Kaplan McLaughlin Diaz

San Francisco, California

In the months following the attack on the World Trade Center, Kaplan McLaughlin Diaz began developing a proposal for the site that involved both planning and programmatic components. The firm envisions a World Learning Center, where classes and research could be undertaken relating to global concerns. The scheme places four to five towers, forty to fifty stories in height, on the east side of Greenwich Street, with the footprints of the former towers left as open space. The towers sit on a base, seven or eight stories high, where highly active center-related functions, such as theaters and classrooms, are located. The towers themselves would be devoted to a mix of residential, office, and research facilities. Although most of the site development has been determined, architect Herbert McLaughlin says he has gotten a warm response from varied universities and is still hoping to convince the LMDC about the need for such a center at Ground Zero.

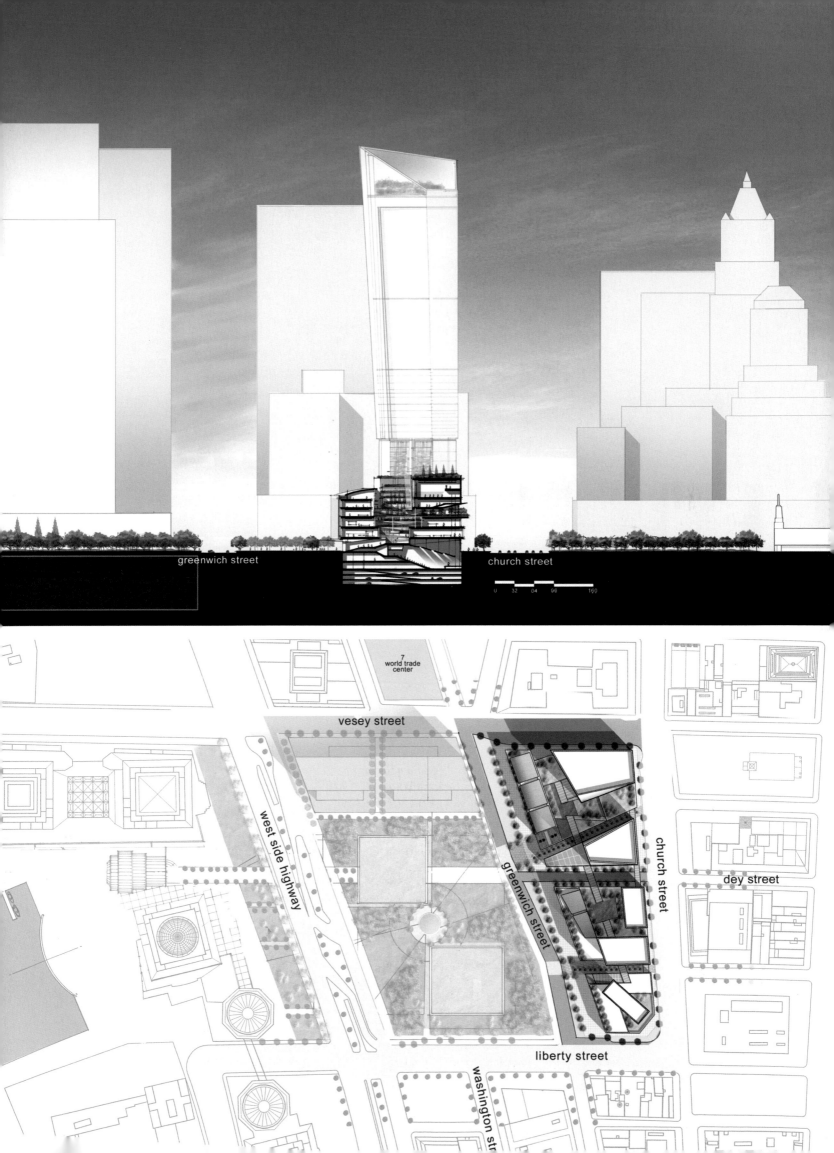

greenwich street

church street

U 32 04 98 160

7 world trade center

vesey street

west side highway

greenwich street

church street

dey street

liberty street

washington str

MEMORIAL

Fred Bernstein

New York City

Two piers, whose dimensions correspond to those of the Twin Towers, extend into New York Harbor from Battery Park, one oriented toward the Statue of Liberty, one oriented toward Ellis Island. Horizontal bands at 12-foot intervals represent the 110 stories of the original towers, and are inscribed with the names of the victims on each floor. The names of rescue workers who lost their lives are also represented prominently.

Mario Gentile

New York City

Two massive blocks of onyx mark the footprints of the original towers, with one block occupying the footprint of the south tower and inscribed with a small memorial to the attack on February 26, 1993. The other onyx block hovers over the footprint of the north tower, supported by a series of aluminum markers, one for each of the victims, whose names are inscribed on the markers. A processional walk leads to a plaza built into the Hudson River, with a memorial garden and a chapel.

Kruunenberg van der Erve

**Gerard Kruunenberg and
Paul van der Erve**

Amsterdam, Netherlands

Twin shafts occupy the footprints of the original towers as mirror images 110 stories deep. At the base of these shafts is located a space for contemplation, reached by elevators that run along the shafts' sides. The two shafts, which have views of the sky, are connected by a corridor that opens onto a staircase leading up to street level.

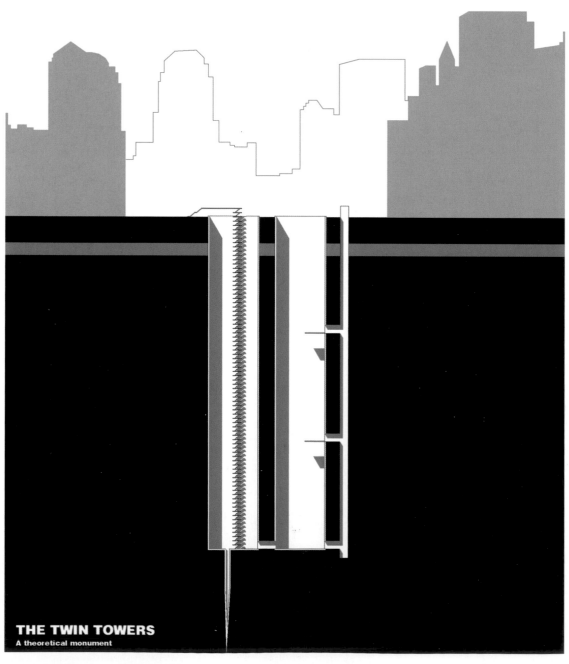

THE TWIN TOWERS
A theoretical monument

Markus Dochantschi

New York City

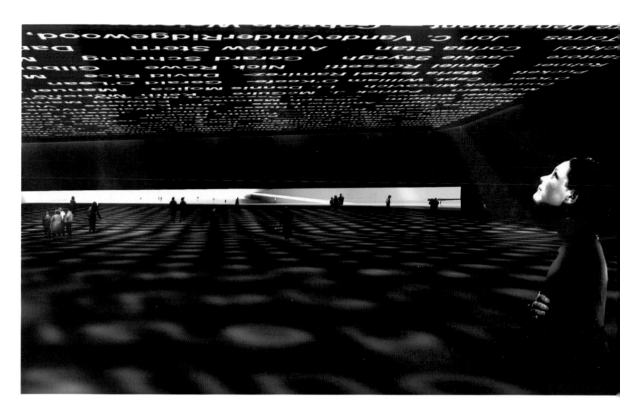

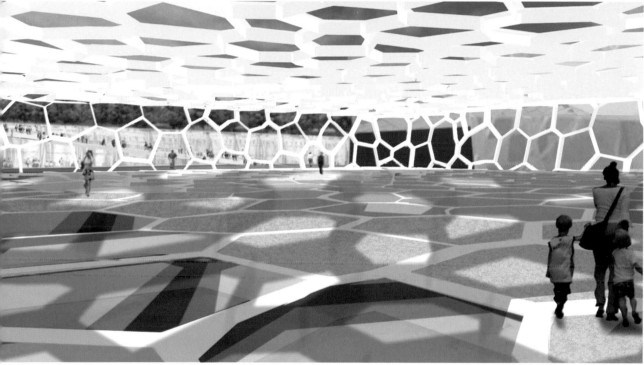

In a scheme submitted to the LMDC memorial competition (fall 2003), architect Markus Dochantschi designed two memorials to each occupy one of the footprints of the original towers. The north memorial comprises a quiet, partially submerged space lit by openings made by carvings of the victims' names into the roof (top). The south memorial comprises 388 components, representing the earth's 388 nations, with each element integral to the structure of the memorial, so that the removal of any one would eventually result in the memorial's collapse (above). The space within this structure rests above a pool of water and serves as a place for contemplation.

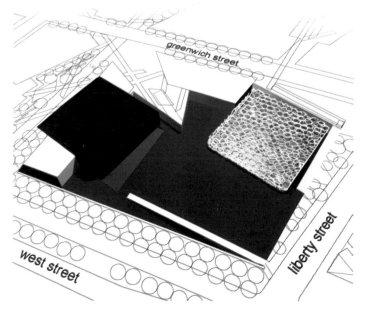

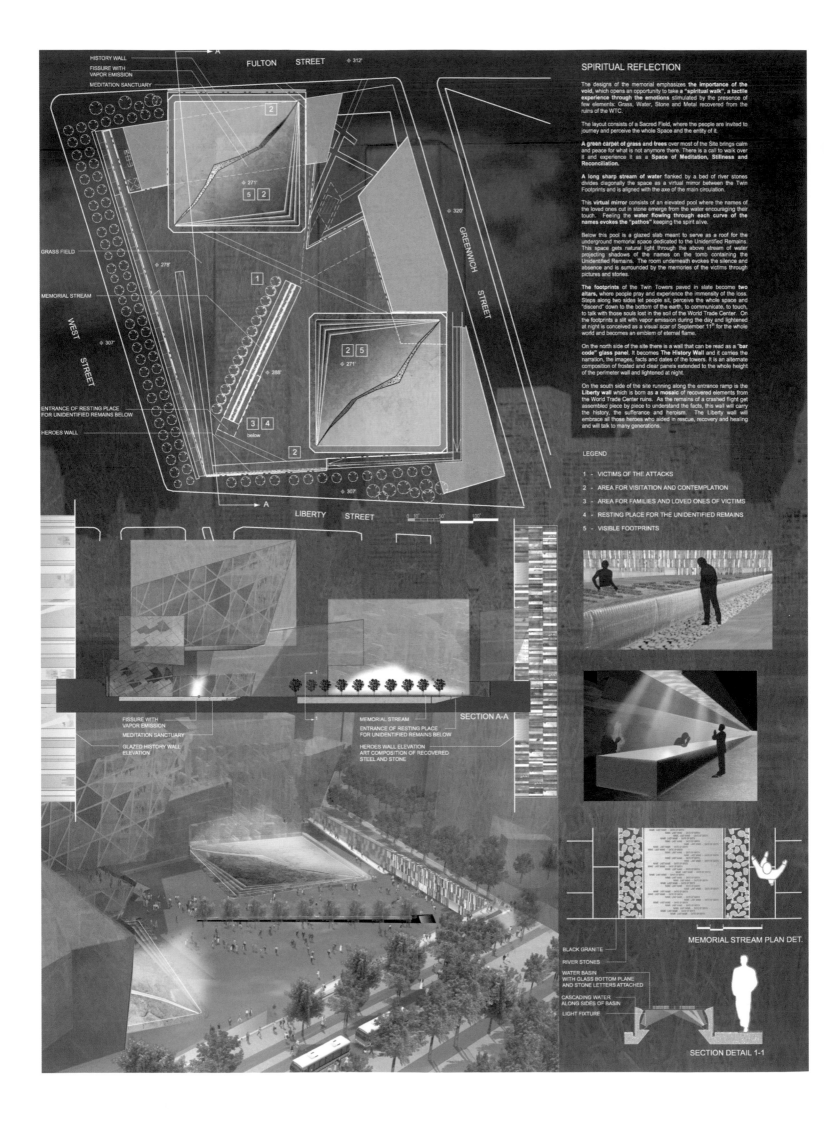

HISTORY WALL
FISSURE WITH VAPOR EMISSION
MEDITATION SANCTUARY

FULTON STREET ◇ 312'

GRASS FIELD

MEMORIAL STREAM

ENTRANCE OF RESTING PLACE FOR UNIDENTIFIED REMAINS BELOW

HEROES WALL

WEST STREET

GREENWICH STREET

◇ 320'

◇ 278'

◇ 271'

◇ 307'

◇ 288'

◇ 271'

below

◇ 307'

LIBERTY STREET

SPIRITUAL REFLECTION

The designs of the memorial emphasizes **the importance of the void**, which opens an opportunity to take a **"spiritual walk", a tactile experience through the emotions** stimulated by the presence of few elements: Grass, Water, Stone and Metal recovered from the ruins of the WTC.

The layout consists of a Sacred Field, where the people are invited to journey and perceive the whole Space and the entity of it.

A green carpet of grass and trees over most of the Site brings calm and peace for what is not anymore there. There is a call to walk over it and experience it as a **Space of Meditation, Stillness and Reconciliation**.

A long sharp stream of water flanked by a bed of river stones divides diagonally the space as a virtual mirror between the Twin Footprints and is aligned with the axe of the main circulation.

This **virtual mirror** consists of an elevated pool where the names of the loved ones cut in stone emerge from the water encouraging their touch. Feeling the **water flowing through each curve of the names evokes the "pathos"** keeping the spirit alive.

Below this pool is a glazed slab meant to serve as a roof for the underground memorial space dedicated to the Unidentified Remains. This space gets natural light through the above stream of water projecting shadows of the names on the tomb containing the Unidentified Remains. The room underneath evokes the silence and absence and is surrounded by the memories of the victims through pictures and stories.

The footprints of the Twin Towers paved in slate become **two altars**, where people pray and experience the immensity of the loss. Steps along two sides let people sit, perceive the whole space and "descend" down to the bottom of the earth, to communicate, to touch, to talk with those souls lost in the soil of the World Trade Center. On the footprints a slit with vapor emission during the day and lightened at night is conceived as a visual scar of September 11th for the whole world and becomes an emblem of eternal flame.

On the north side of the site there is a wall that can be read as a **"bar code" glass panel**. It becomes The History Wall and it carries the narration, the images, facts and dates of the towers. It is an alternate composition of frosted and clear panels extended to the whole height of the perimeter wall and lightened at night.

On the south side of the site running along the entrance ramp is the **Liberty wall** which is born as a **mosaic** of recovered elements from the World Trade Center ruins. As the remains of a crashed fight get assembled piece by piece to understand the facts, this wall will carry the history, the sufferance and heroism. The Liberty wall will embrace all those heroes who aided in rescue, recovery and healing and will talk to many generations.

LEGEND

1 - VICTIMS OF THE ATTACKS

2 - AREA FOR VISITATION AND CONTEMPLATION

3 - AREA FOR FAMILIES AND LOVED ONES OF VICTIMS

4 - RESTING PLACE FOR THE UNIDENTIFIED REMAINS

5 - VISIBLE FOOTPRINTS

FISSURE WITH VAPOR EMISSION
MEDITATION SANCTUARY
GLAZED HISTORY WALL ELEVATION

MEMORIAL STREAM
ENTRANCE OF RESTING PLACE FOR UNIDENTIFIED REMAINS BELOW
HEROES WALL ELEVATION
ART COMPOSITION OF RECOVERED STEEL AND STONE

SECTION A-A

MEMORIAL STREAM PLAN DET.

BLACK GRANITE
RIVER STONES
WATER BASIN WITH GLASS BOTTOM PLANE AND STONE LETTERS ATTACHED
CASCADING WATER ALONG SIDES OF BASIN
LIGHT FIXTURE

SECTION DETAIL 1-1

Rossana Capurso, Sudhir Bhatia, Lory Laera

New York City

For their scheme submitted to the LMDC memorial competition (fall 2003), a team of three designers was cited by Julie Iovine in the *New York Times* (February 1, 2004) for taking an original approach to the use of water. At the center of a green space is an elevated reflecting pool: at its bottom a glass slab admits light into an underground memorial for unidentified victims. The slab also is incised with the names of the victims, which cast shadows into the space below. The footprints of the original towers are surfaced in slate and function as informal "altars" where people can gather in remembrance. Each of the footprints is marked by fissures, or "scars," that emit vapor during the day and light in the evening.

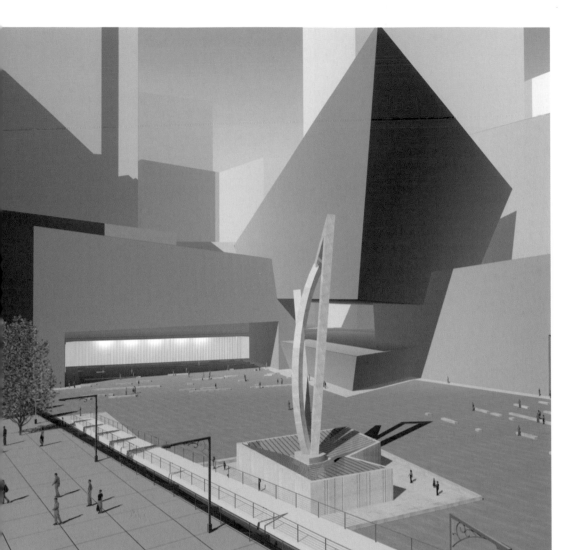

MEMORIAL

Arthur Carter/Centerbrook

New York City

In fall 2003, Arthur Carter, the publisher of the *New York Observer*, in conjunction with the Connecticut architectural firm Centerbrook, proposed a stainless steel sculpture on a granite base to be located between the footprints of the original towers. At the base is a stainless steel tomb for the unidentified victims. The footprints themselves contain randomly situated stone benches, and the names of the victims are carved into metal walls around the sunken site.

Youngsun Ko, Adam Sokol

New York City and New Haven, Connecticut

The introduction of giant white pines onto the site symbolically embodies the spirit of growth and resolve in a proposal described as an "optimistic gesture" by its architects, students at Yale University. Amid this urban forest of pines is a series of glass pylons, each one representing a victim of the attacks, radiating from the two footprints of the original towers (site plan, below). The radial organization of the trees' axes can extend to outlying areas that wish to show solidarity by planting their own white pines.

Michael Sorkin Studio

New York City

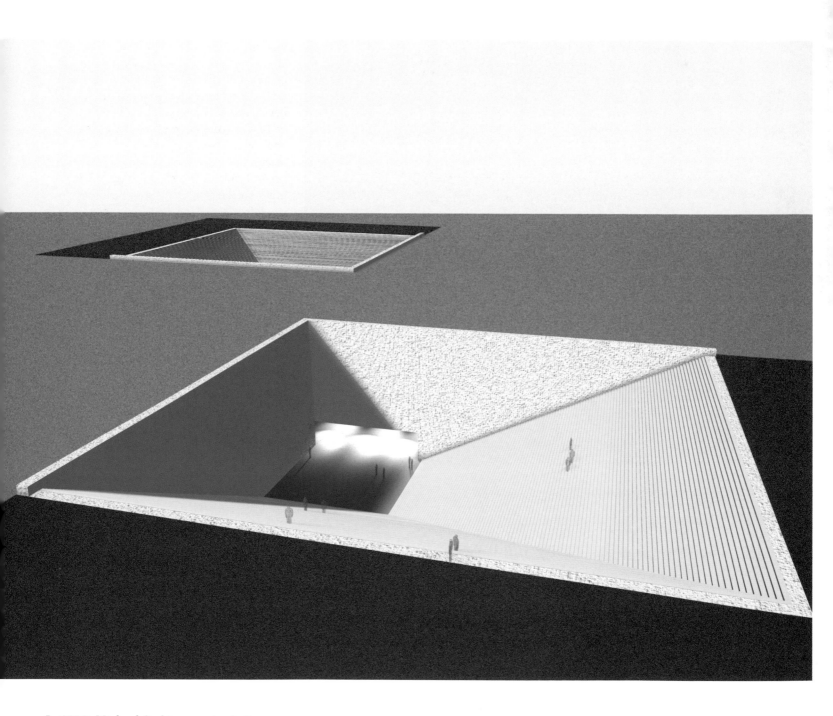

In 2002, Michael Sorkin conceived of a scheme with two monumental staircases at the footprints of the original towers descending 72 feet to the level of bedrock on the site. The entire area of the footprints is open overhead. The footprints are connected below ground by a memorial hall—where the names of the victims are inscribed—which occupies the area directly between the two footprints.

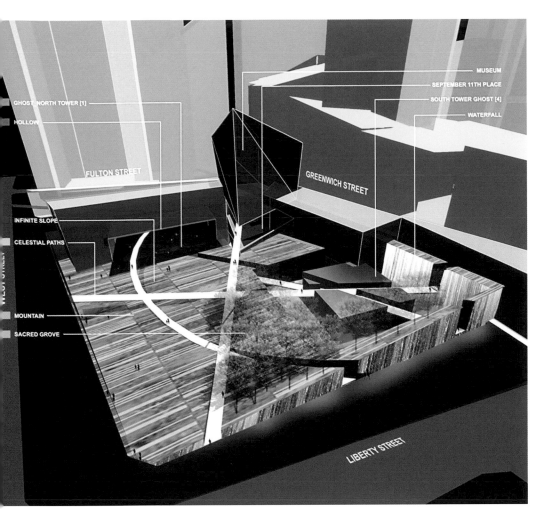

MUSEUM
SEPTEMBER 11TH PLACE
SOUTH TOWER GHOST [4]
WATERFALL

GHOST NORTH TOWER [1]
HOLLOW

FULTON STREET
GREENWICH STREET

INFINITE SLOPE
CELESTIAL PATHS

MOUNTAIN
SACRED GROVE

LIBERTY STREET

NOMADE Architecture

Michel Lauzon, Martin Leblanc, Jean Pelland

Montreal, Quebec

A submission to the memorial competition (fall 2003), this scheme followed its parameters with a Dantesque descent and ascent. The site is conceived as a tilted plane, and the footprints of the original towers receive radically different treatments in this spatially complex scheme. The footprint of the north tower is sunken at the site's deepest end and contains a space with a floor inscribed with the victims' names, the incisions of which illuminate a space below. The south tower's footprint is occupied by a cubic form situated in a pool and functioning as a tomb for the unidentified victims.

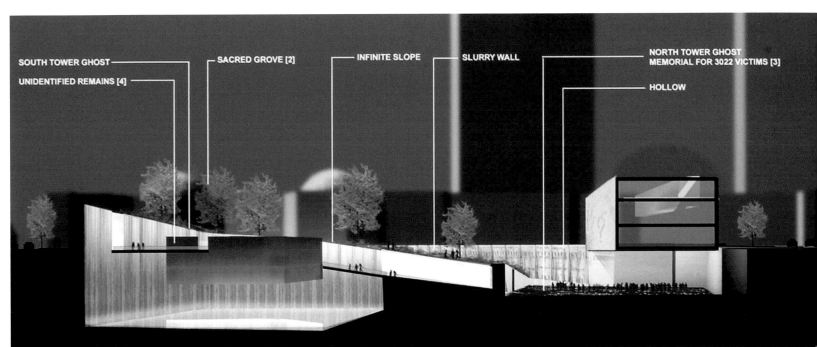

SOUTH TOWER GHOST
UNIDENTIFIED REMAINS [4]

SACRED GROVE [2]

INFINITE SLOPE

SLURRY WALL

NORTH TOWER GHOST
MEMORIAL FOR 3022 VICTIMS [3]

HOLLOW

Miró Rivera Architects

Juan Miró, Miguel A. Rivera

Austin, Texas

An arc of 3,016 bronze columns represents the estimated number of victims of the terrorist attacks on the World Trade Center in 1993 and 2001. Each of the columns' heights corresponds to the age of the person whose name is inscribed there. At the north end, a building serves as a space for contemplation and as a final resting place for the unidentified victims. The footprints of each of the original towers are marked by 10-foot-wide moats, with bridges offering access to a lawn and plaza spaces. At the south end is a 140-foot-long, 40-foot-tall "Weeping Wall," which will serve as a ceremonial backdrop.

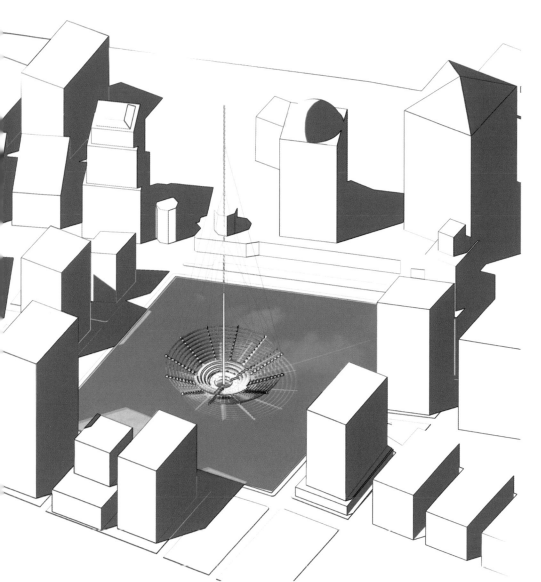

Miró Rivera Architects

Juan Miró, Miguel A. Rivera

Austin, Texas

A reflecting pool occupies the entire World Trade Center site, with a bowl-shaped structure located in the center of the pool. The structure contains burial space both for those who lost their lives in the attacks and for those who would simply choose the site as their final resting place. A mast emerging from this "necropolis" rises to the full height of the original towers, with an eternal flame at its apex.

Macrae-Gibson Architects

Gavin Macrae-Gibson

New York City

Submitted to the open memorial competition, Gavin Macrae-Gibson's scheme shows a sloping plane dominating the north side of the site. A monumental steel marker from the wreckage of the World Trade Center sits on the slope, which functions as a park and as a ramp leading from street level down to a reflecting pool in the footprint of the south tower. The pool's floor features images of the victims. A list of their names is located in a memorial hall under the north slope, etched into a bronze interactive console: when a visitor touches the console, the selected name appears in large format on a random arrangement of glass plates.

MEMORIAL

Patricia Nieto

Minneapolis, Minnesota

A master's thesis project executed in fall 2001 and spring 2002 at the University of Minnesota's College of Architecture and Landscape Architecture, the International Global Memorial is a series of monuments located on the sidewalks of cities around the world. These small interventions are composed of one heavy, permanent wall made of local materials and featuring recesses where visitors can place flowers, mementos, etc. A lighter, nearly transparent wall projects live images from each of the memorials around the world. To create a sense of separation from the surrounding environment, each memorial is approached by descending into a lower ground plane.

Nicholas de Monchaux, Kathryn Moll de Monchaux, Omar Rabie

New York City

Antonio Gaudí as proposed by Paul Laffoley

Barcelona, Spain; Boston, Massachusetts

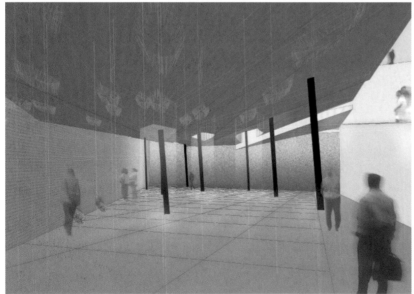

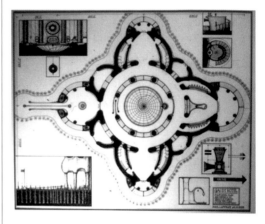

In January 2003, architect Paul Laffoley proposed finally constructing at the World Trade Center site a hotel tower designed by Antonio Gaudí in 1908. Originally intended to be built in lower Manhattan, the tower rises to a height of 1,048 feet. An interior cavern 412 feet high—which was originally to contain slots representing every U.S. president up to the year 3000—would function as a memorial space for the victims of the attacks. Though bizarre by many standards, Laffoley's proposal to erect what was intended as a sort of love letter to New York is also rather touching.

Composed of two hundred boats, modeled after nineteenth-century skiffs, this scheme suggests a reconciliation of New York past and present as a way of healing. A meadow shaped to resemble ocean waves supports the boats, which are oriented out toward the Verazzano Narrows, implying movement into the greater world. Each of the boats bears the name of approximately a dozen victims of the attacks, and at night lamps placed at the tops of their masts illuminate the site, which becomes a sea of light.

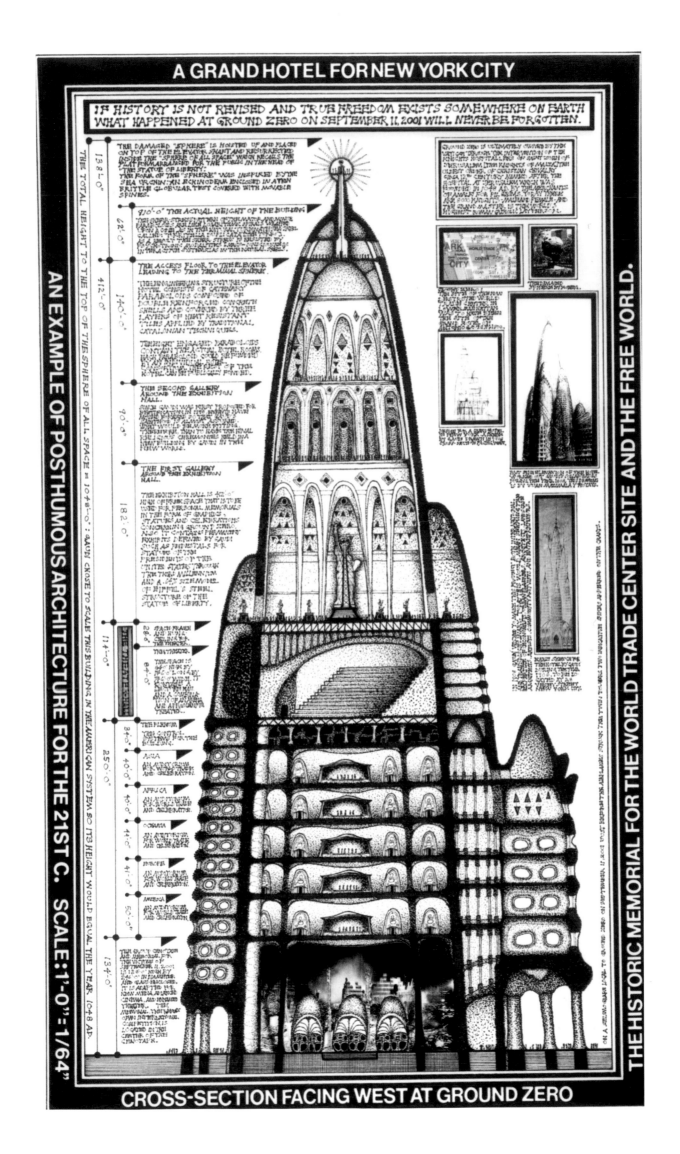

A GRAND HOTEL FOR NEW YORK CITY

IF HISTORY IS NOT REVISED AND TRUE FREEDOM EXISTS SOMEWHERE ON EARTH WHAT HAPPENED AT GROUND ZERO ON SEPTEMBER 11, 2001 WILL NEVER BE FORGOTTEN.

AN EXAMPLE OF POSTHUMOUS ARCHITECTURE FOR THE 21ST C.   SCALE:1'-0":1/64"

THE HISTORIC MEMORIAL FOR THE WORLD TRADE CENTER SITE AND THE FREE WORLD.

CROSS-SECTION FACING WEST AT GROUND ZERO

Bibliography

Architectural Record
October 2001 to March 2004

(only opening pages are given)

Amelar, Sarah. "A New York Exhibition Looks toward the Future of the World Trade Center Site." Vol. 190 (March 2002): 59.

Campbell, Robert. "A Better Piece of New York Will Be the Truest Memorial to the World Trade Center Tragedy." Vol. 189 (December 2001): 37.

———. "Advice to Architects: Keep Howard Roark and His Grand Schemes Away from Ground Zero." Vol. 190 (August 2002): 59.

———. "Instead of Devising a 21st-Century Urbanism, the Latest WTC Proposals Rehash Old Notions of the Future." Vol. 191 (February 2003): 75.

Czarnecki, John E. "All 140 Mancini Duffy Employees Survive WTC Disaster Unscathed, Back to Work in Three Days." Vol. 189 (October 2001): 26.

———. "Architects that Worked near World Trade Center Return to Practice, Keeping Data Off-site." Vol. 189 (November 2001): 35.

———. "Gensler Assists 24 WTC Clients Find New Space, Become Operational Again." Vol. 189 (November 2001): 33.

———. "National Building Museum Hosts Events in Terror Aftermath." Vol. 189 (November 2001): 42.

———. "Engineers Further Study Structural Failures in World Trade Center." Vol. 189 (December 2001): 21.

———. "First Downtown N.Y.C. Building Completed Post 9/11 Opens." Vol. 190 (January 2002): 28.

———. "As Cleanup Continues, Planning Process for WTC on Fast Track." Vol. 190 (February 2002): 28.

———. "Heavily Damaged Buildings Surrounding Ground Zero Require Extensive Renovations." Vol. 190 (March 2002): 26.

———. "New York Remembers with Two Temporary Memorials." Vol. 190 (April 2002): 28.

———. "Planning Moves Quickly on 7 WTC and Other Components." Vol. 190 (April 2002): 30.

———. "Report on WTC Collapse Leaves More Questions than Definitive Answers." Vol. 190 (June 2002): 28.

———. "Urban Design Team to Develop WTC Land-Use Plan by Year End." Vol. 190 (June 2002): 26.

———. "Beyer Blinder Belle Partners Talk to Record about Momentous Undertaking—The Lower Manhattan Plan." Vol. 190 (July 2002): 23.

———. "SOM Designs WTC Skyscraper for Silverstein." Vol. 190 (July 2002): 23.

———. "Initial WTC Plans Raise Process, Program, and Vision Questions." Vol. 190 (August 2002): 23.

———. "Clarifying WTC Plan Designers." Vol. 190 (September 2002): 36.

———. "Opening WTC Planning Process Adds More Questions to Mix; Memorial Design Competition to Come in 2003." Vol. 190 (September 2002): 36.

———. "New York Architecture Critics Select Favorite Designers to Develop Plans for WTC Site." Vol. 190 (October 2002): 35.

———. "Waiting for Ground Zero." Vol. 190 (December 2002): 26.

———. "Architects at the Forefront as They Show Ground Zero Aspirations." Vol. 191 (February 2003): 31.

———. "Libeskind and THINK Move Forward in Process to Design WTC Site." Vol. 191 (March 2003): 29.

———. "Task Force Recommends Stringent Codes for N.Y.C. Buildings." Vol. 191 (March 2003): 36.

———. "Libeskind Design Chosen for WTC Site, but Process and Time-Frame Questions Remain." Vol. 191 (April 2003): 33.

———. "Politics and Legalities Now Focus for WTC." Vol. 191 (May 2003): 40.

———. "Registration Started and Jury Named for WTC Memorial Competition." Vol. 191 (May 2003): 40.

———. "Progress, Setbacks at WTC Development." Vol. 191 (June 2003): 28.

Dean, Andrea Oppenheimer. "Panelists: Despite Terrorist Attack, the Skyscraper Is Here to Stay." Vol. 189 (December 2001): 21.

Deitz, Paula. "Down at the WTC: Dissident Thoughts amid the Fanfare and Boosterism." Vol. 192 (February 2004): 53.

Giovannini, Joseph. "Will Libeskind's Plan for the World Trade Center Site Become a Massive Design Swap?" Vol. 191 (April 2003): 89.

Gorlin, Alexander, and John E. Czarnecki. "Unlikely Collaboration of Architects Design Viewing Platform." Vol. 190 (February 2002): 26.

Hart, Sara. "In the Aftermath of September 11, the Urban Landscape Appears Vulnerable and Random." Vol. 190 (March 2002): 135.

Ivy, Robert F. "Lanterns and Light Catchers." Vol. 189 (October 2001): 34.

———. "Renzo Piano Speaks with Record about Skyscrapers and the City: Piano Comments on the WTC Disaster." Vol. 189 (October 2001): 136.

———. "Shaking off the Terror." Editorial. Vol. 189 (October 2001): 21.

———. "Where Do We Go from Here?" Editorial. Vol. 189 (December 2001): 15.

———. "The Case for a Competition." Editorial. Vol. 190 (May 2002): 23.

———. "Outside the Lines." Editorial. Vol. 190 (August 2002): 15.

———. "One Year Later." Editorial. Vol. 190 (September 2002): 19.

———. "One Out of Nine?" Editorial. Vol. 191 (February 2003): 21.

———. "An Open Letter to David Childs and Daniel Libeskind." Editorial. Vol. 191 (August 2003): 19.

———. "Hurry Up and Wait." Editorial. Vol. 192 (January 2004): 16.

Knecht, Barbara. "Infrastructure Is Valuable Real Estate, Too." Vol. 190 (June 2002): 156.

Lerner, Kevin. "Yamasaki's World Trade Center Boasted an Embattled, Remarkable History." Vol. 189 (October 2001): 27.

———. "Architect Creates Map to Orient Ground Zero Visitors." Vol. 190 (February 2002): 28.

———. "World Trade Center Images and Proposals at Biennale." Vol. 190 (June 2002): 30.

———. "Rebuild the WTC Towers? Death of the Skyscraper? Architects and Engineers Weigh In." Vol. 190 (October 2002): 25.

———. "Student Studios Address WTC Plans." Vol. 190 (October 2002): 68.

———. "Six Unique Teams of World-Renowned Architects Selected to Develop Design Proposals for World Trade Center Site." Vol. 190 (November 2002): 28.

———. "R.Dot Recommends New Retail Corridors in Lower Manhattan." Vol. 191 (March 2003): 30.

———. "Libeskind, Port Authority Agree on Transit Hub; Environmental Review Process Begins for WTC." Vol. 191 (July 2003): 25.

———. "Libeskind and Silverstein Reach an Agreement for WTC Site." Vol. 191 (August 2003): 27.

Linn, Charles. "Fear Must Not Become a Form-Giver for Architecture." Vol. 190 (March 2002): 55.

Lubell, Sam. "An Interview with Daniel Libeskind." Vol. 191 (September 2003): 36.

———. "An Interview with David Childs." Vol. 191 (September 2003): 36.

———. "On Track: Calatrava Joins WTC Team." Vol. 191 (September 2003): 35.

———. "WTC Briefs." Vol. 191 (September 2003): 35.

———. "An Interview with Kevin Rampe." Vol. 191 (October 2003): 26.

———. "Libeskind's 'Refinements' Include Slimmer Tower." Vol. 191 (October 2003): 25.

———. "Original WTC Models on Display in Washington, D.C." Vol. 191 (October 2003): 25.

———. "Significant Progress at WTC Accompanied by Building Boom in Lower Manhattan." Vol. 191 (October 2003): 25.

———. "Corbin Building Will Be Saved." Vol. 191 (November 2003): 25.

———. "Foster, Nouvel, and Maki Join WTC Team." Vol. 191 (November 2003): 25.

———. "Interview with Monika Iken." Vol. 191 (November 2003): 26.

———. "Interview with Robert Tierney." Vol. 191 (November 2003): 26.

———. "Silverstein Loses Initial Insurance Bid." Vol. 191 (November 2003): 25.

———. "Tsien Resigns from LMDC Board." Vol. 191 (November 2003): 25.

———. "Governor Moderates as Architects Tangle over Freedom Tower." Vol. 191 (December 2003): 19.

———. "Memorial Finalists Named." Vol. 191 (December 2003): 19.

Acknowledgments

———. "World Trade Center Station Finished." Vol. 191 (December 2003): 19.

———. "WTC Memorial Finalists' Designs." Vol. 191 (December 2003): 20.

———. "Freedom Tower's Design Unveiled." Vol. 192 (January 2004): 23.

———. "Grimshaw and Arup Working on Fulton Street Transit Station." Vol. 192 (February 2004): 21.

———. "Inside the Jury: An Interview with James Young." Vol. 192 (February 2004): 24.

———. "Memorial Gets Price Estimate." Vol. 192 (February 2004): 21.

———. "New York New Visions Joining LMDC Team." Vol. 192 (February 2004): 21.

———. "Progress at Ground Zero." Vol. 192 (February 2004): 22.

———. "Reflecting Absence Chosen as World Trade Center Memorial." Vol. 192 (February 2004): 21.

———. "An Interview with WTC Memorial Designer Michael Arad." Vol. 192 (March 2004): 24.

———. "Design for World Trade Center Transit Hub Unveiled." Vol. 192 (March 2004): 23.

———. "Insurance Trial Continues." Vol. 192 (March 2004): 23.

———. "JFK Link Options Announced." Vol. 192 (March 2004): 23.

———. "Plan for WTC Cultural Complex Released." Vol. 192 (March 2004): 23.

Mellins, Tom. "Symposium Looks to the Grands Travaux for Inspiration in Rebuilding Lower Manhattan." Vol. 190 (November 2002): 40.

Pasnik, Mark, with John E. Czarnecki. "Plans Move Rapidly on Temporary Commuter Train Station at WTC Site; More Firms in Mix." Vol. 190 (December 2002): 26.

Rogers, Christina V. "Young Firms Adjust to a Changed City." Vol. 189 (November 2001): 59.

Russell, James S. "Debating the Future of the World's Financial Capital." Vol. 189 (November 2001): 47.

———. "Alexander Garvin, the Top Planner for WTC Redevelopment, Talks about Process, Vision." Vol. 190 (May 2002): 43.

———. "Who Owns Grief?" Vol. 190 (July 2002): 120.

———. "LMDC and Port Authority Agree to Develop WTC Plan by End of January, and Mayor Bloomberg Presents His Own Vision." Vol. 191 (January 2003): 34.

———. "SOM Designs New Silverstein Tower for 7 WTC Site." Vol. 191 (January 2003): 34.

Russell, James S., and John E. Czarnecki. "Multiple Interests and Agendas Compete for Attention in Lower Manhattan." Vol. 190 (May 2002): 42.

Snoonian, Deborah. "Intricate WTC Cleanup to Continue for Months." Vol. 189 (November 2001): 33.

———. "Forensics Engineering Expert Studying WTC Steel to Determine Precisely How Towers Failed." Vol. 190 (January 2002): 26.

———. "Contest Hopes to Spur Green Development around Ground Zero." Vol. 191 (October 2003): 26.

Snoonian, Deborah, and John E. Czarnecki. "Local Engineers Rush to Assist Removal." Vol. 189 (October 2001): 27.

———. "World Trade Center's Robust Towers Succumb to Terrorism." Vol. 189 (October 2001): 22.

———. "WTC Neighboring Buildings Inspected; Some Require Extensive Reconstruction." Vol. 189 (November 2001): 35.

Sokol, David. "With Lessons Learned from 9/11, New York Plans Building-Code Changes for High-Rises." Vol. 190 (September 2002): 50.

———. "Winter Garden $50 Million Reconstruction Completed One Year after 9/11 Destruction." Vol. 190 (October 2002): 37.

———. "Closed Since 9/11, Office to Be Cleaned of Contaminants." Vol. 190 (November 2002): 30.

Sorkin, Michael. "Making Lists: the Byzantine Politics of Picking Design Firms for Ground Zero." Vol. 190 (November 2002): 63.

———. "Can Architects and Planners Use Security Concerns to Create More Humane Cities?" Vol. 191 (March 2003): 73.

———. "Where Are the Visionary Architects Who Can Plan New Cities Now That We Need Them?" Vol. 191 (May 2003): 105.

———. "Obstructed Vision: Constraints Limit WTC Memorial Even before Design Is Selected." Vol. 191 (July 2003): 57.

Stephens, Suzanne. "Architects without Architecture at Ground Zero." Vol. 190 (July 2002): 124.

———. "Do Recent Collaborations of Design Architects for the WTC Site Show That Gropius Had It Right?" Vol. 191 (March 2003): 65.

Taylor, Tess. "Architects Assemble and Catalog WTC Artifacts for History." Vol. 190 (March 2002): 28.

Weathersby Jr., William. "Significant Damage to Subways near WTC." Vol. 189 (November 2001): 34.

Whitehead, Ingrid. "F. Joseph Moravec: A Man with a Mission." Vol. 189 (October 2001): 268.

Much of the information for the accounts of the official process (the Lower Manhattan Development Corporation and the Port Authority of New York and New Jersey) and the unofficial presentation organized by the Max Protetch Gallery is based on articles published in *Architectural Record*. Writers appearing in *Record* include author Suzanne Stephens, as well as John Czarnecki, Sam Lubell, James Russell, Michael Sorkin, Robert Campbell, Joseph Giovannini, Sarah Amelar, Sara Hart, Deborah Snoonian, Kevin Lerner, Charles Linn, William Weathersby, and Ingrid Whitehead. Additional writers on the topic appear in the bibliography. We should also like to thank Julie Iovine for her invaluable advice, along with Allen Prusis for his suggestions. Ford Peatross of the Library of Congress, and Stuart Krimko of the Max Protetch Gallery were particularly solicitous of our needs, and we owe special thanks to Diana Lind and Nicholas Olsen for their assistance.

Illustration Credits

All illustrations on the following pages, courtesy Lower Manhattan Development Corporation (LMDC): 26, 36, 39 bottom, 40, 41, 42, 43, 44, 45, 46. 47. 54, 55, 56, 57, 58, 59, 60, 61, 62, 63, 64, 65, 66, 67, 68, 69, 70, 71, 72, 73, 74, 75, 76, 77, 78, 79, 81, 82, 83, 84, 85, 86, 87, 88, 89, 90, 91, 92, 93, 96, 97, 98, 99, 100, 101

All other images appear courtesy of the architects, except for the following:

Dorothy Alexander, 10

Architectural Record, 29

Bettman/Corbis, 18, 19 top

Blandon Belushin, 96–99

Canadian Centre for Architecture, 15 top

dbox: 37, 38, 39 top

Lindsay Farrell, 19 bottom

Balthazar Korab, 20, 21 top, 132 top

Sam Lubell, 49

The Museum of Modern Art, New York, 12, 13; digital image © The Museum of Modern Art/Licensed by SCALA/Art Reserve, NU, The Museum of Modern Art, New York, 14

Jock Pottle, 32, 36, 90, 91, 100, 101

Thorsten Siedel, 55, 56, 64 bottom

sQuared design lab: 39 bottom, 40

Lara Swimmer/ESTO, 15 bottom

Ramin Talaie, 8, 9, 52, 53, 94

Team Twin Towers, 24

Courtesy of Paul Willen, 22, 23

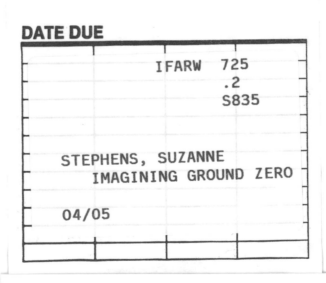